RON RANDALL'S TREKKER™ OMNIBUS

DARK HORSE BOOKS

Cover Illustration **RON RANDALL WITH JEREMY COLWELL**

President and Publisher **MIKE RICHARDSON**
Original Series Editors **RANDY STRADLEY AND DIANA SCHUTZ**
Collection Editor **JIM GIBBONS**
Collection Designer **IRINA BEFFA**

TREKKER OMNIBUS

This volume reprints material previously published in Dark Horse Presents *Vol. 1 #4–#6, #20–#22, and #39–#41,* Trekker *#1–#6,* Trekker Color Special, *and* A Decade of Dark Horse *#2, originally published by Dark Horse Comics; and* Trekker *#1, originally published by Image Comics.*

Published by Dark Horse Books
A division of Dark Horse Comics, Inc.
10956 SE Main Street
Milwaukie, OR 97222

DarkHorse.com

International Licensing: (503) 905-2377
To find a comics shop in your area, call the Comic Shop Locator Service toll-free at (888) 266-4226.

First edition: August 2013
ISBN 978-1-61655-211-4

10 9 8 7 6 5 4 3 2 1
Printed in China

CONTENTS

FOREWORD

Here's the thing about revolutions.

Sometimes, they're tricky.

Sometimes, we don't even know they're happening at the time, and it's only later, with more context, that we get to really see where the foundations were laid.

So it is with this character, this series, you are about to read. *Trekker* is about a female bounty hunter, Mercy St. Clair, a take-no-feces, take-no-prisoners genuine badass in an often-steamy science-fiction setting with more than a heap of noir detective fiction thrown in for good measure.

I was a kid when this book came out, but I was fascinated by the black-and-white comics revolution. Something was clearly happening; almost overnight, all the buzz in comics seemed to focus on the next noncolored property by creators I'd never even heard of.

It was a wonderful, exciting time for comics, but it carried over some of the things I'd found annoying in the mainstream books . . . Many of even the very best titles still seemed aimed squarely at a male audience, and female characters with their own agency still seemed to be a tiny minority. Frustrating, that this seismic change was happening, and we were still thinking of females as a fringe readership, almost a collection of unicorns, as rare as misprinted postage stamps.

Trekker took a different approach entirely. The lead character was beautiful, but she was also fully clothed. She was an object of lust for many a thug around her, but she quickly taught them the meaning of respect, and maybe even a little fear.

She was, as I said, a badass.

A female badass, the lead in her own series, the fulcrum upon which the stories were balanced. Smart, tough, dedicated, cool as ice, and hot as a freshly fired pistol—there had been damn few characters like her in all media, and in comics she was damn near without precedent.

I liked her immediately.

Trekker happened almost a decade before Xena. My son, he's never known a time without Ripley or Lara Croft or Buffy, but there was a time when any *hint* of a tough female adventure heroine was a scarcity and an oddity we in the female readership were begging for.

It's of stuff like *Trekker* that revolutions are begun. A female character that is sexy but not sexualized, that is tough but not without flaws and doubts, and that is dangerous but not without compassion.

It's a good job that the stories are still good fun, a nice sense of grim, day-to-day reality in a setting where morality has to change as technology outpaces evolution. And Ron's art is top notch, of course, but you already knew that, I'm sure. I was fortunate enough to work with him briefly on some *Wonder Woman* issues . . . Unsurprisingly, he nailed them. A tough, smart, female badass warrior?

Turns out that was familiar territory to Ron.

I like this character and this series a lot. Thank you, Mr. Randall, for being ahead of the game when I wanted it most.

—Gail Simone

P.S. More *Trekker*, please.

***Gail Simone** is a multiple-award-winning writer of comics and animation, with critically acclaimed runs on* Wonder Woman, Birds of Prey, Deadpool, Batgirl, *and many other titles. She lives on the Oregon coast with her husband and two weird dogs.*

TREKKER
R. RANDALL

Story and art
RON RANDALL

Colors
JEREMY COLWELL

Lettering
DAVID JACKSON

Chapter break art
RON RANDALL

NEW GELAPH. FHAH!
I'VE HAD IT WITH THIS DUMP TOWN.
SHUT UP AND DEAL, FAZL.
AW, I MEAN IT. ARE WE UPPOSED TO SIT HERE OOLING OUR HEELS VAITING FOR THAT FAT--
HEY!
YOU'RE NEW, FAZL. SO THIS TIME THAT TALK WON'T COST YOU A LUNG. FAIR WARNING.
HUH! THIS GATEFISH CLOWN HAS ALL YOU GUYS SPOOKED. I TELL YA--
O! I TELL OU-- UT UP R I'LL--
hink!
TREKKER
by RON RANDALL
WELL, WELL! LOOKS LIKE SOME-ONE'S WANDERED INTO THE WRONG PART OF TOWN! BUT -- LONG AS YOU'RE HERE, SUGAR, LET'S --
EASY, FAZL -- CHECK OUT HER HARDWARE--
CHAPTER 1
LETTERED BY DAVID JACKSON

"... SHE'S A TREKKER."
NOBODY HAS TO DIE HERE. I JUST NEED SOME INFORMATION.
GATEFISH HAS A BIG "MEETING" TONIGHT. WHERE AND WHEN?

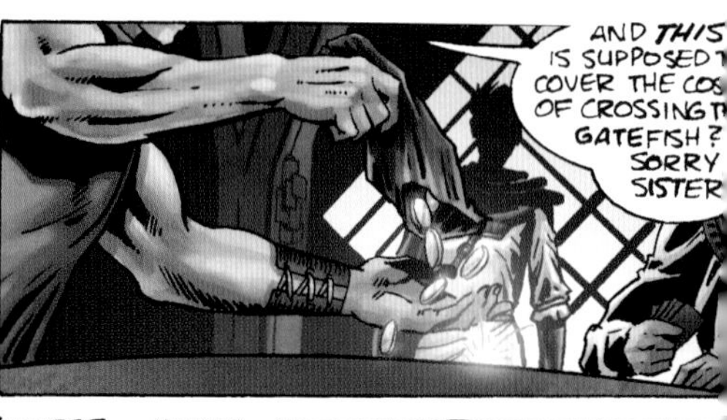
AND THIS IS SUPPOSED T COVER THE COS OF CROSSING T GATEFISH? SORRY SISTER

'COURSE--MAYBE YOU GOT SOMETHING ELSE YOU COULD SWEETEN THE POT WITH, EH, HONEY?
SURE...
FAZL--

...YOUR LIFE.
I MAKE A GOOD CLEAN PULL ON THE .34 AND IT REALLY SETS THE PUNK BACK ON HIS HEELS. IF IT WAS HIS CHOICE, WE COULD WOR THIS OUT...

...BUT I CAN TELL THE OTHERS ARE GOING TO FORCE THE ISSUE.
THE PUNK KNOWS IT TOO.
n-no...

TAKE HER OUT!
THOOM!

AKE MY LIVING BRINGING IN KILLERS, SCRUFFERS, BURNLINERS, WHAT HAVE YOU...

LIVE OR
D, THE PAY'S
SAME.

STOP HOWLING, FAZL...

YOU'RE RED ZONE, SURE. BUT WITH PROPER CARE, YOU CAN STILL PULL THROUGH.

PROMPT, COURTEOUS MEDICAL ATTENTION IS ONLY A CALL AWAY.

TALK TO ME AND I'M A SAMARITAN.

UNDER THE... BLUE HORN...

MIDNIGHT.

IT'S ENOUGH.

3.

THE COPS ARRIVE FORTY MINUTES LATER, TRYING TO LOOK IN CONTROL.

NO ONE'S BEEN IN CONTROL IN THIS CITY FOR TWENTY YEARS. THAT'S WHY *TREKKERS* KEEP GETTING PAID.

FOUR DEAD, ONE CRITICAL. HERE'S YOUR RECEIPT, MERCY.

THANKS.

THIS GATEFISH, MERCY. HE'S BIG LEAGUE. ALREADY DRESSED OUT THREE TREKKERS. THREE THAT WE'VE I.D.'D, ANYWAY. THEY WERE IN PIECES, MERCY. LITTLE PIECES.

LOOK, I KNOW COPS AND TREKKERS GOT LITTLE USE FOR EACH OTHER. BUT I'M ASKING FOR YOUR OWN SAKE AS WELL AS OURS -- STAY CLEAR OF THIS ONE.

JUST DISAPPEAR FOR A WHILE, MERCY. LET US DO OUR JOB.
THANKS FOR THE RECEIP

MERCY'S JUST LIKE EVERYBODY ELSE. SHE STOPPED LISTENING TO COPS YEARS AGO. MOSTLY, EVEN *I* DON'T BLAME HER.

SHE LIVES DOWN IN ANTARI ALLEY. NOT MUCH OF A NEIGHBORHOOD.
TARI APTS

NOT MUCH OF A PLACE, EITHER. I KNOW. I'VE BEEN THERE A FEW TIMES. MOST OF WHAT A TREKKER MAKES GOES INTO ORDNANCE.

I THINK SHE'S STILL GOT SCUF, THOUGH.
GUESS HE'S ABOUT ALL SHE'S GOT LEFT FROM THE OLD DAYS...

...BACK WHEN A "BATTLE" WAS A WRESTLING MATCH WITH THAT PUP.

AND BLOOD WAS NOTHING MORE THAN A SCRAPED-UP KNEE.

THOSE DAYS ARE JUST MEMORIES FOR MOST OF US NOW...
... I WONDER IF MERCY REMEMBERS THEM AT ALL...

5.

MIDNIGHT... UNDER THE BLUE HORN...
THE BLUE HORN

GATEFISH IS PROMPT AT LEAST. HE LUMBERS AROUND WAITING FOR HIS CONTACT, LIKE HE OWNS THE WHOLE TOWN. LIKE HE DOESN'T HAVE A SYSTEMSWIDE PRICE ON HIS HEAD.

BUT I WON'T POP HIM YET. IF I WAIT FOR BOTH HIM AND HIS PARTNER, THE REWARD'S BOUND TO BE--
FREEZE, TREKKER.

NOT A TWITCH-- OR YOU'RE ONE DEAD BOUNTY HUNTER.
SENSORS PICKED HER UP LIKE A CHARM, HUH, CLANE?
SHUT UP, RAKKEN.
STRIP OFF HER HARDWARE. GATEFISH'LL LOVE THIS.
SENSORS -- AND GRAV HARNESSES! HOW DID A GOON LIKE GATEFISH HOOK INTO THIS KIND OF HIGH TECH?
THE POSSIBLE ANSWERS ARE ALL DISTURBING, BU I'LL HAVE TO SAVE THEM FOR LATER--
IF I HAVE A LATER!

HEY, BOSS! CHECK OUT THIS ACTION!
SO-- THAT FOOL FAZL DID TALK TO HER.
CLANE-- HAVE A MAN ON THE FORCE TAKE CARE OF FAZL, WILL YOU?
RIGHT. UH, SAY, BOSS...
HOW ABOUT GIVING RAKKEN AND ME A LITTLE R&R TIME WITH THIS HERE? WE BEEN GOOD BOYS!
HUMPF! RESTRAIN YOURSELF, CLANE...
... KNOWING YOU ANIMALS, THERE'D BE NOTHING LEFT OF HER. NO -- I HAVE SOMETHING MORE CONSTRUCT IN MIND FOR OUR STUNNING LITTLE TREKKER.

FOR NOW, JUST GAS HER AND GET HER OUT OF SIGHT BEFORE MY BUSINESS PARTNER ARRIVES. YOU KNOW HOW TOUCHY HE CAN BE.

CONSIDER IT DONE, BOSS.

KAY, DOLL FACE. AVE A WHIFF.

THE *FUMES* HIT AND MY BRAIN NUMBS ALMOST INSTANTLY. FIRST-CLASS MATERIAL AGAIN. *GATEFISH* IS DEFINITELY A TOP-DRAWER ACT. AS THE BLACK WAVE SWALLOWS ME, I WONDER IF I AM...

LATER, THERE'S THE ROARING IN MY EARS...

... THEN THE STRONG GRIPS ON MY ARMS AND LEGS, THE WIND THAT'S BLOWING IN MY FACE...

...THEN I OPEN MY EYES...

AH! WELCOME BACK! YOU'RE JUST IN TIME FOR THE "SHOW"-- WHICH IS GOOD, SINCE YOU ARE TO BE THE *STAR*!

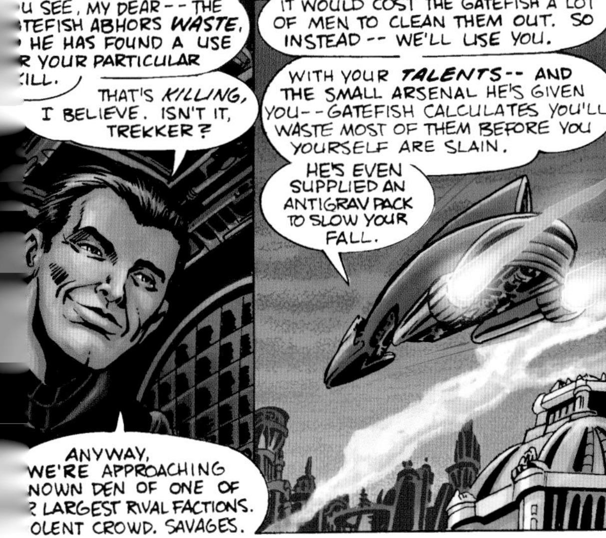

U SEE, MY DEAR-- THE TEFISH ABHORS *WASTE*, HE HAS FOUND A USE R YOUR PARTICULAR ILL.
THAT'S *KILLING*, I BELIEVE. ISN'T IT, TREKKER?
ANYWAY, WE'RE APPROACHING NOWN DEN OF ONE OF LARGEST RIVAL FACTIONS. OLENT CROWD. SAVAGES.
IT WOULD COST THE GATEFISH A LOT OF MEN TO CLEAN THEM OUT. SO INSTEAD -- WE'LL USE YOU.
WITH YOUR *TALENTS*-- AND THE SMALL ARSENAL HE'S GIVEN YOU--GATEFISH CALCULATES YOU'LL WASTE MOST OF THEM BEFORE YOU YOURSELF ARE SLAIN.
HE'S EVEN SUPPLIED AN ANTIGRAV PACK TO SLOW YOUR FALL.

HE'S A GENIUS, DON'T YOU THINK?
GO TO HELL.

SHOULDN'T BE AT ALL SURPRISED.
ALL RIGHT, BOYS--DROP HER--*NOW*!
7.

THAT SKYLIGHT... IT'S MY ONLY CHANCE...

WHICH MUST MEAN...

IT'S RIGHT WHERE THEY WANT ME!
CRAAAASH

A TREKKER!

DUST HER!

"TREKKER" continues in PART 2.

GATEFISH STRAUSS IS DEFINITELY HIGH ON MY BLACKLIST.
HE'S WORKED IT SO THAT, INSTEAD OF ME COLLECTING THE SIZABLE BOUNTY ON HIS HEAD, I'M CLEANING OUT HIS UNDERWORLD COMPETITION TO SAVE MY OWN SKIN.
IN MY LINE OF WORK, YOU HAVE DAYS, AND THEN YOU HAVE DAYS.
TREKKER
Chapter 2
WRITTEN AND ILLUSTRATED BY RON RANDALL
LETTERED BY WORKMAN-
AT LEAST THESE "TRINKETS" FROM GATEFISH SHOULD EVEN THE ODDS A BIT.
K-12 SHOCK LAUNCHERS...
...AGAIN I WONDER WHERE GATEFISH GETS ALL THIS PRIME HARDWARE.
9

WITH A LITTLE TIME, I'M SURE I COULD PIECE IT TOGETHER...
...BUT JUST NOW, TIME IS SOMETHING I'M SHORT ON...
IN FACT, I THINK I'D BEST BE GOING...
THERE SHE--
WHAT--?
SMOKE BOMBS!
KRUMP
KRUMP
DOORWAY.
FA-TOOM
NOW WHERE?
DOES IT MATTER?
JUST MOVE YOUR FEET...
...AND HOPE THEY DON'T--
HEY! UP HERE!

SHH! THEY WON'T--
WHUUU
QUICK! THIS WAY!
UH. SORRY.
THAT'S... ALL RIGHT. I HAVE OTHER RIBS.
WHEW!
YOU'RE A REAL FIRE-CRACKER, LADY.
JUST HAT ARE OU DOING I HERE? OU A OP?
O. BUT I AM ERE UNDER COVER.
EN URE A EKKER, O.
HA HA! NO, NO, I'M NOT A TREKKER. IN FACT, I WORK FOR RIGEL.
RIGEL? WHAT'S RIGEL?
YOU'VE NEVER HEARD OF RIGEL? WELL, PERHAPS NOT. YOU'RE PRETTY REMOTE OUT HERE.
BUT THERE'S NO TIME FOR THAT NOW. THEY'LL BE DOUBLING BACK SOON.
COME ON.
11

WHERE?
YOU WANT TO GET OUT OF HERE, DON'T YOU?
LEAD ON.

I DON'T TRUST THIS JOKER FOR A MINUTE. BUT I FIGURE IF HE CROSSES ME, I CAN ALWAYS KILL HIM.
shh.
FISSK

CHOK

WHAP

VERY PRETTY.
SAY, HOW'D YOU GET IN THIS FIX, ANY-WAY?
I CROSSED A GANG-STER NAMED GATEFISH. HE--
NEVER MIND. I'VE HEARD OF HIM.
I'M GOING TO GET HIM.
NOT ALONE YOU WON'T.
THIS WAY...
YOU'RE GOOD, BUT YOU'D NEED HELP.
I KNOW. THERE'S A COP I CAN USE.
A COP? DOESN'T GATEFISH OWN--
I CAN TRUST THIS ONE.
IT'D BETTER BE WITH YOUR LIFE.
GARAGE. THERE'LL BE THREE OR FOUR INSIDE.
I, UH, DON'T SUPPOSE YOU'D LIKE A HAND WITH THEM...?
BAM
GOOD EVENING. ANY CHANCE OF ME GETTING A LIFT FROM ONE OF YOU GENTS?
WHA-- BLAST HER!
BRAKA BRAKA
TZING
BEEOW
13

WELL, THAT'LL BRING THE GANG OF THEM. YOU'D BEST TAKE OFF.
GOOD LUCK WITH GATE-FISH. BE CAREFUL WHO YOU TRUST.
LOOK, WHY ALL THIS ADVICE?

I JUST WANT YOU TO BE IN ONE PIECE THE NEXT TIME WE MEET.
"NEXT TIME"? YOU GET THAT FROM A CRYSTAL BALL?
NOPE! DON'T NEED ONE! GOOD-BYE, "FIRE-CRACKER."

...RIGHT. GOOD-BYE, "SPACE-CASE."
EVERY DAY I ARRIVE AT THE STATION, IT'S LIKE I NEVER LEFT...
THREE NEW MURDER
SEVEN DEAD-END
BURNLINER LEAD
AND TWO RIOTS
BREWING, AND NO
THE MANPOWER TO
HANDLE ANY OF IT.

IT'S LIKE TRYING TO WARD OFF A SUPERNOVA WITH SUNSCREEN.
MORNING, LIEUTENANT.
UH-HUH.

AND THAT'S NOT TO MENTION THE DRU RUNNERS, THE SMUGGLERS, TH MISSING PER-SONS, LIKE...

...MERCY!
CLOSE THE DOOR.
I CAN'T BELIEVE IT! I THOUGHT GATEFISH MUST HAVE--
HE TRIED. NOW IT'S MY TURN. WIL YOU HELP

I DO..
NEVER SAY DIE, HUH, MERCY? OKAY, FOR WHAT IT'S WORTH, COUNT ME IN.
YOU HAVE SOMETHING IN MIND?

WE'LL SET ME UP AS A TARGET. ONE HE'LL HAVE TO COME AFTER HIMSELF.
WELL, THE TARGET PART'LL BE EASY. SOON AS HE HEARS YOU'RE STILL ALIVE...
...HE'LL ORDER YOU HIT...

...BUT HOW CAN WE MAKE SURE HE'LL COME HIMSELF?
WITH THIS...

GATEFISH "LENT" THIS TO ME. WHAT DO YOU MAKE OF IT?

NICE PIECE.
"NICE"? THAT'S GOVERNMENT TECH. IT HAS TO BE.
WHICH CONFIRMS A THEORY I HAVE: HE'S GOT SOMEONE FROM THE COUNCIL IN HIS POCKET.

FILE. HOW
CAN'T YOU GUYS PUT TWO AND TWO TOGETHER?
WHAT DO YOU THINK WE'VE BEEN TRYING TO DO?
BUT WE'VE NEVER HAD ANY HARD EVIDENCE--

WELL, NOW WE HAVE. JUST LET IT OUT THAT I'M ON TO GRAY. HE'LL COME.
HE WOULDN'T TRUST HIS GOONS ON SOMETHING LIKE THIS.
15

NOW I'VE GOT TO GO BEFORE SOMEONE SPOTS ME IN HERE. IF WORD OF OUR LITTLE CHAT GOT TO GATEFISH...

RIGHT-- SO MUCH FOR OUR TRAP.

OKAY, MERCY. FOR GATEFISH I CAN DRAW A FEW MEN. BUT YOU KNOW THE RISKS. HE'S GOT PLENTY OF COPS IN HIS POCKET, TOO...

...MAYBE EVEN *ME*. YOU THOUGHT OF THAT, MERCY?

I'VE THOUGHT OF IT.

"TREKKER" conclude in part three.

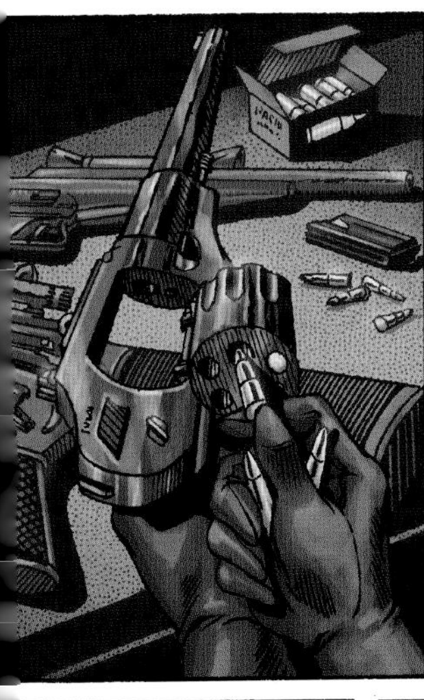
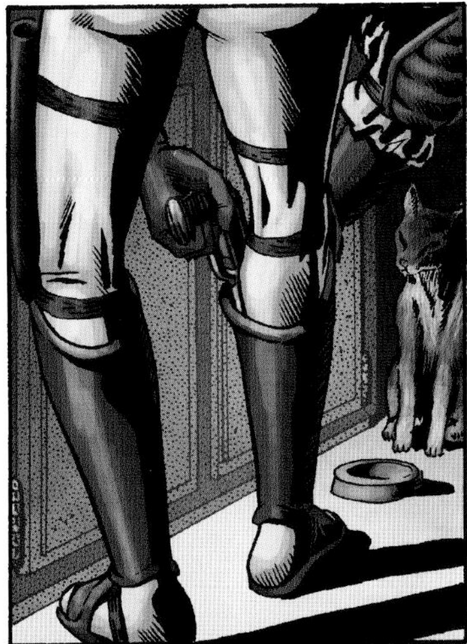
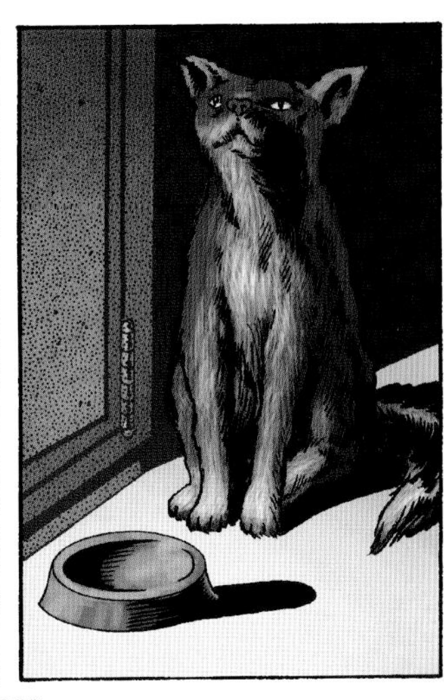
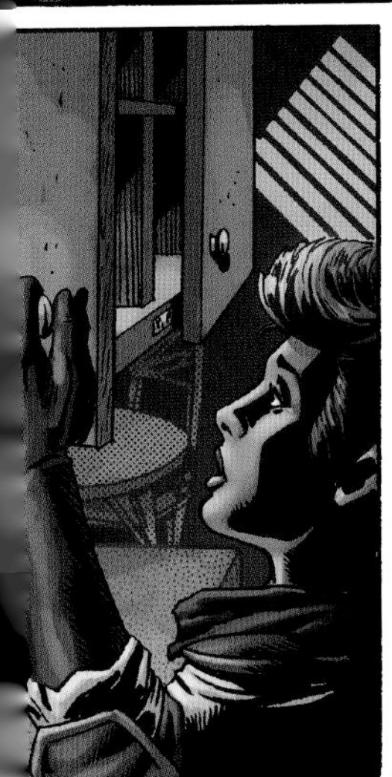
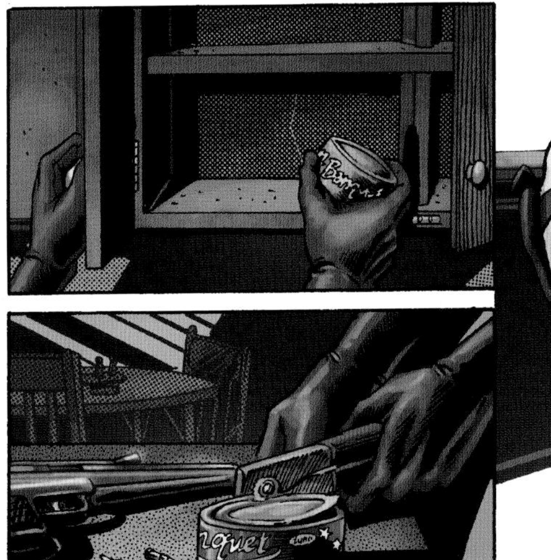
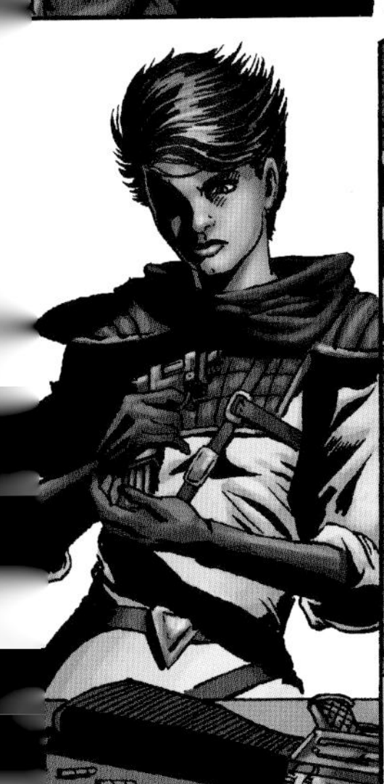
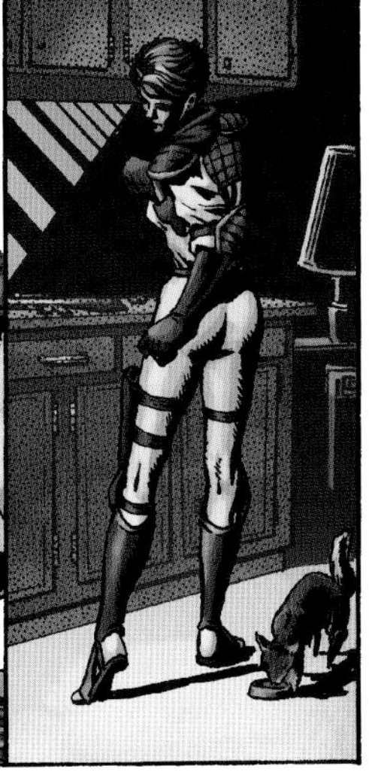
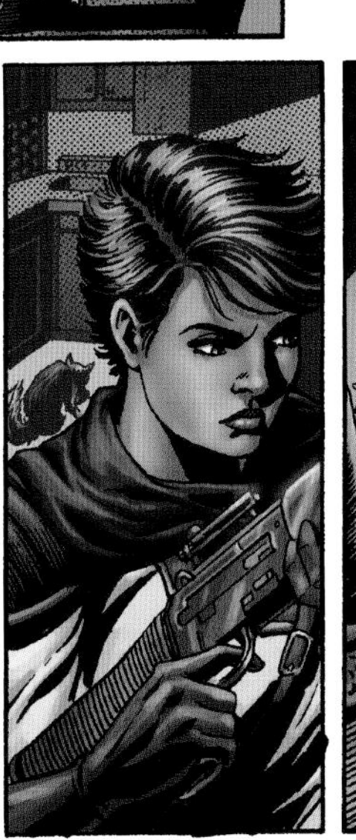
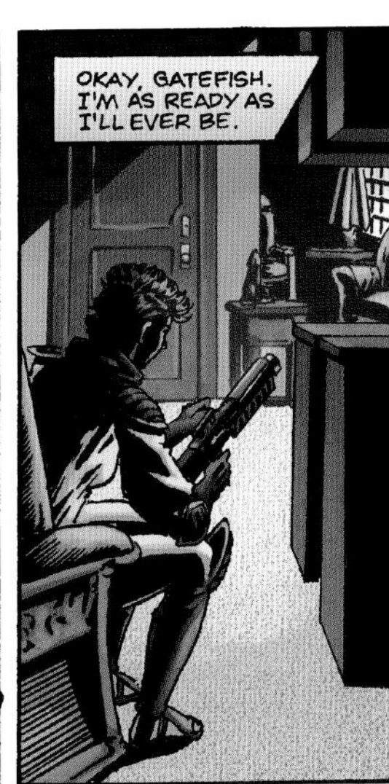

OKAY, GATEFISH. I'M AS READY AS I'LL EVER BE.

17

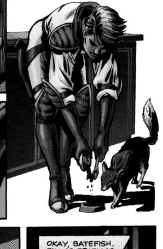

I KNEW THAT ONCE ***UNCLE ALEX*** LET OUT THE RUMOR THAT I'D CONNECTED HIM WITH COUNCILMAN GRAY, GATEFISH WOULD COME AT ME SOON. BUT THIS IS PRETTY QUICK. ALSO A LITTLE ***OBVIOUS***. I'D EXPECTED MORE FROM THE GREAT GATEFISH STRAUSS. GUESS ANYONE CAN MAKE A MISTAKE.

YAAAA!

MOLLY!

TREKKER

Chapter 3

by RON RANDALL

LETTERED BY DAVID JACKSON

MOLLY... MY GOD. WHAT ARE YOU DOING HERE? I ALMOST...
DAMN IT! YOU'RE SUPPOSED TO COME ON *WEDNESDAYS!*
I... I *DID* COME WEDNESDAY! BUT YOU WEREN'T HERE SO I THOUGHT I'D CHECK ON SCUF AGAIN TODAY.
I BROUGHT THESE FOR HIM.
I WAS *WORRIED* ABOUT YOU, MERCY. YOUR LINE OF WORK DOES THAT TO FRIENDS, Y'KNOW.
LOOK, MOLLY... I'M SORRY. YOU HAVE TO LEAVE. NOW. SOMETHING—
RIGHT. "SOMETHING VERY BIG..." I'M NOT *BLIND,* MERCY.
YOU KEEP SHOOTING FOR A GGER AND BIGGER CKPOT. BUT SOME Y ONE OF THEM ST MIGHT *BLOW UP* IN YOUR *FACE.* AND—
MOLLY...
RIGHT. WHAT DO *I* KNOW? I'M JUST A SHOPKEEPER.
OODBYE, MOLLY.
BE CAREFUL, MERCY.
CLATCH

LADY'S COMIN' BACK OUT, LIEUTENANT. YOU WERE RIGHT: FALSE ALARM.
INTARI APTS
uh-huh. WHEN GATEFISH *DOES* MAKE HIS MOVE, WE'LL BE *LUCKY* TO CATCH IT.

19

I HIT THE STREETS RIGHT ON SCHEDULE, TAKING MY USUAL ROUTE THROUGH THE CRANCH-VENDOR ALLEYS. I MAKE IT EASY FOR GATEFISH.
I SURE HOPE UNCLE ALEX IS UP THERE LIKE HE'S SUPPOSED TO BE.
JAINS— GET READY TO MOVE TO—
KA-REEEEE
WHAT IN—?
REEEEEEEEE
JEEZ, LIEUTENANT—! SHALL I CALL IN A—
WHERE'S MERCY?
I CAN'T SEE—
IT'S A DECOY!
"JAINS! CAN YOU—"
TOO LATE.

AND HOPE WE'LL BE IN TIME.
MISS MERCY ST. CLAIR. WE MEET AGAIN. THAT IS *UNUSUAL* FOR MY ENEMIES.
YOU'RE VERY RESOURCEFUL. BUT YOU'VE MADE THIS LITTLE TRAP TOO *EASY*. I KNOW YOU HAVE *FRIENDS* OUT THERE. POLICE, OR OTHER TREKKERS.
I ASSURE YOU THEY CANNOT HELP YOU.
IT'S PITCH BLACK, SO ALL I CAN DO IS GO FOR THE SOUND OF HIS VOICE.
BLAM
KPOW
AAAGH!
DON'T WASTE
TIME, MISS ST.
MY MEN ALL HAVE
YOU'LL
HAVE TO LISTEN.
THE ONLY THING THAT'S KEEPING YOU ALIVE, YOU KNOW, IS THE POSSIBILITY THAT YOU HAVE SECRETED AWAY CERTAIN *INFORMATION* THAT I AM... CONCERNED ABOUT.
INFRAREDS, HUH?
IF YOU *DO* HAVE THIS INFORMATION, YOU MUST TELL ME WHERE IT IS NOW.
YEAH? WHAT'D KEEP ME *ALIVE* THEN?
COME ON, PAL... LET'S USE THAT *POLE* AGAIN.
I APPRECIATE YOUR DILEMMA. I'M AFRAID YOU'LL JUST HAVE TO... *TRUST* ME, MY DEAR.
21

SHIK
THERE!
SORRY, GATEFISH. NO DEAL.
WHUUH!
WHACK
MOSSEL! CHANCH! ALL OF YOU--GET HER-- BUT ALIVE!
CHOK
WHUMP
KRACK
SMACK

MOSSEL! CHANCH!–
–WHAT'S–
YOU KEEP TAKING CHANCES WITH ME, YOU SLUG...
YOUR MISTAKE.
GAAAA!

WE'VE GOT A TRACK ON YOU, MERCY. BE RIGHT THERE.
BRING MEDICAL.
YOU NEVER DID HAVE THE INFO ON ME... DID YOU? YOU'RE A CLEVER CHILD.
WELL. VERY GOOD FOR YOU. THEY'LL NEVER HOLD ME, OF COURSE. SO, YOU'LL KILL ME NOW?

NO? I MUST SAY I'M DISAPPOINTED. IT SEEMS AT YOUR CORE YOU'RE WEAKER THAN I THOUGHT.
WHAT IS IT? PRINCIPLES? MORALS? FAH! WHO EVER HEARD...OF A MORAL BOUNTY HUNTER?

YOU CAN'T HAVE IT BOTH WAYS, MISS ST. CLAIR. ONE DAY... YOU'LL SEE THAT. THEN YOU'LL EITHER... WAKE UP ... OR GIVE UP.

YOU'RE A REGULAR PHILOSOPHER, AREN'T YOU, GATEFISH?

23

HEY, LIEUTENANT! THEY'RE DOWN HERE! SHE'S ALL RIGHT AND SHE'S GOT GATE-FISH!
HE WAS OUT IN TWO WEEKS. "SOME-BODY UPSTAIRS PULLED STRINGS," THEY SAID. MERCY AND I BOTH KNEW WHO...
THAT'S THE GAME, MERCY. BUT DON'T WORRY, COUNCILMAN GRAY WILL SLIP UP SOONER OR LATER.
AT LEAST GATEFISH WAS SET BACK A BIT. NOT MUCH VICTORY, BUT...
DON'T WORRY, UNCLE ALEX. I GOT THE "HEAD MONEY." AT LEAST I WON'T RUN OUT OF AMMO FOR A WHILE...
...AND NEITHER WILL SCUF!
MERCY SMILED. I LAUGHED. WE WERE CELEBRATING. WE WERE STILL ALIVE. THAT, TOO, WAS ONLY A SMALL VICTORY. BUT IN THIS TOWN, YOU TAKE WHAT YOU CAN GET.
end

SMUGGLER'S BLUES

Story and art
RON RANDALL

Lettering
KEN BRUZENAK

Chapter break art
RON RANDALL

THEY SAY IF YOU LIVE IN NEW GELAPH LONG ENOUGH, YOUR BLOOD TURNS AS GRAY AS THE GRIT THAT FILLS THE AIR, GRIMES THE BUILDINGS, AND TAINTS THE WATER.

WELL, IN MY WORK, I'VE SEEN A *LOT* OF BLOOD. AND *IT'S* ALL BEEN RED.

ENJOY Ceek

STILL, I KNOW WHAT THEY MEAN. IT'S NOT A TOWN THAT ENCOURAGES YOUR HOPE OR YOUR FAITH...

...NOT IN THE SOCIETY...

...NOT IN YOUR NEIGHBORS...

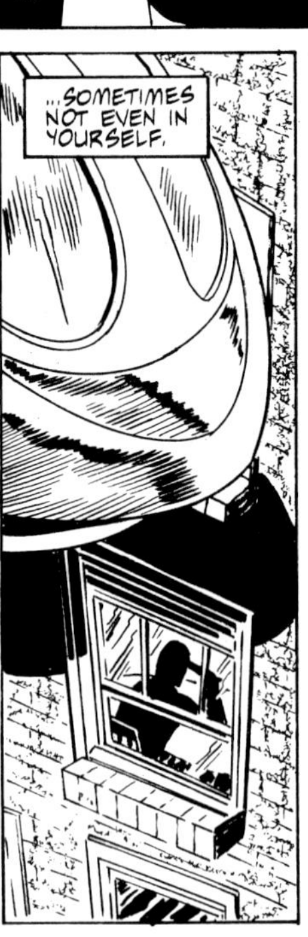

...SOMETIMES NOT EVEN IN YOURSELF.

I'M A TREKKER. MY NAME IS MERC ST. CLAIR, AND THIS IS MY HOMETOWN.
RIGHT HERE, BRAKMAN. OF COURSE I MADE IT...

...IT'S ALWAYS EASY TO SLIP INTO A RATHOLE TOWN LIKE THIS ONE.
THAT'S WHAT THE P.U.A. IS FIGHTING TO CHANGE, ISN'T IT?
RIGHT. MIKKA WILL TAKE CARE OF THE SHIP. LET'S GET YOU OUTTA HERE.

TAKE IT EASY. THE COPS HERE CAN'T FIND THEIR OWN--
FREEZE, YOU TWO-- POLICE!
WELL--IT'S STRAVIN, ISN'T IT? GOT A LITTLE CONTRABAND COMING INTO THE FAIR WALLS OF NEW GELAPH, HUH?
THAT'LL NEVER DO. HAVE TO BRING YOU IN...

UNLESS, OF COURSE, YOU'D CARE TO PAY THE SPECIAL TARIFF...?

HAH. SEE, BRAKMAN? JUST LIKE I WAS TELLING YOU. REASONABLE COPS HERE IN NEW GELAPH.
HERE, OFFICER. THIS SHOULD COVER IT.
YEAH... THIS'LL DO NICELY.

I'LL HAVE TO CALL IN THIS "ABANDONED VEHICLE," BUT YOU'RE FREE TO ENJOY YOUR VISIT, MR. STRAVIN.
2

HUUUWH--

GOOD WORK, MIKKA. CAN'T AFFORD TO LET ANYTHING STOP OUR--

DAMN!

HE HAD A PARTNER!
BWHAM
BWAM
BWAM

I'VE GOT THE CASE. LET'S--
HOLD IT.

OKAY. NOW WE GO.

TOO BAD ABOUT MIKKA.
HE DIED FOR THE CAUSE. WHEN THE CITY IS OURS, HE'LL BE CANONIZED.
Smuggler's Blues
ttered by KEN BRUZENAK
4

BZZZZZT
TWENTY-THIRD PRECINCT. DETECTIVE HALUR...
DENSIN-- I'VE GOT THE REPORT FOR LT. St. CLAIR. WHO'S IN THERE WITH HIM?
THAT'S HIS NIECE, MERCY. BUT GO ON IN. HE'LL WANT THAT REPORT.
WANTED
WANTED
WANTED
NOTICE
Lt. HALUR
WOW. THAT'S HIS NIECE? SHE SURE LOOKS--
YEAH. BUT FORGET IT. SHE'S A TREKKER, OF ALL THINGS.
YOU'RE KIDDING. WHAT A WASTE.
SORRY, MERCY. BUT YOU KNOW AS MUCH AS I DO NOW.
IT WAS STRAVIN'S SHIP IN THE ALLEY. BUT WHAT HE'S BROUGHT IN, WHAT THE ACTION IS, WE STILL DON'T KNOW.
I'LL KEEP YOU UPDATED, THOUGH. FOR THIS JOB, I DON'T CARE WHO BRINGS HIM IN-- COP OR TREKKER.
WELL, FOR THE ©20,000 THE COUNCIL'S PUT ON HIS HEAD, I CARE, UNCLE ALEX.
KNOCK
LIEUTENANT, WE'VE GOT AN I.D. ON THE PUNK IN THE ALLEY. HE-- SORRY--
IT'S ALL RIGHT, LANGSTROM. GO AHEAD. THIS IS MY NIECE...

...MERCY St.CLAIR. MERCY, THIS IS DETECTIVE LANGSTROM. HE'S JUST JOINED US AT THE 23rd.
DETECTIVE.
THE PLEASURE IS MINE, MISS St.CLAIR.

THE REPORT, LANGSTROM...?
RIGHT. THE PUNK WAS A SMALL-TIMER NAMED MIKKA.
NEW GELA

GRAVIS MIKKA?
UM... YES. GRAVIS.
YOU KNOW HIM, MERCY?

JUST HEARD OF HIM.
GOODBYE, UNCLE ALEX. I'M SORRY ABOUT THE TWO YOU LOST.
THANK YOU, MERCY.
GOOD-BYE, MISS St.CLAIR.

MERCY! HEY, MERCY-- HOLD UP.
WHAT IS THIS, MERCY? I HAVEN'T HEARD FROM YOU IN--
PAUL, LISTEN..
LET'S FACE IT-- THEY WERE RIGHT. A COP AND A TREKKER ARE NEVER GOING TO WORK.
OH, WHAT A LINE! COME ON, MERCY. WE HAVE SOMETHING HERE.
SOMETHING STRONG! SOMETHIN REAL.
WHAT WE HAVE ARE THINGS TO DO. YOU HAVE YOURS, I HAVE MINE. GOODBYE, PAUL.
PAUL IS A NICE GUY. A LITTLE SENSITIVE FOR A COP, THOUGH.

VOLCANO ALLEY IS A CHOKING DEN OF FILTH. THE AIR IS THICK WITH SWEAT AND STEAM. THERE IS NO SAFETY IN SHADOW OR IN LIGHT...
...IT'S THE KIND OF PLACE WHERE I DO MY BEST WORK.
ANOTHER WHISKEY, VLATZ. NOW, WHERE WAS I...?
VLATZ BAR

OH, YEAH, SO, SMEDSKI, RIGHT? SMEDSKI SAYS TO HIM, "NO, YOU GIVE ME THE FIVE HUNDRED. SHE'LL NEVER KNOW THE DIFFERENCE!"

HAW HAW HAW!

BUT SHE FINDS OUT, OF COURSE, AND--

HEY, LAZMUSI...

...READY FOR THAT SHOT YOU ORDERED?

SOMETIMES A TOUCH OF **CHEAP DRAMA** IS THE MOST EFFECTIVE **APPROACH**.

HERE, FOR INSTANCE, IT'S KEEPING THIS ROOM FULL OF JACKALS AT BAY. BUT IT WON'T HOLD THEM LONG.

LONG TIME NO SEE, LAZMUSI. LET'S TAKE A WALK, SHALL WE?

WHATEVER YOU SAY, St. CLAIR. IT'S YOUR CALL-- FOR NOW.

HEARD ABOUT YOUR FRIEND MIKKA?

JUST GOT HIS TICKET PUNCHED IN SOME ALLEY WORKING FOR STRAVIN.

VLATZ BAR

I *WANT* STRAVIN. YOU'LL TELL ME WHERE I CAN FIND HIM.

I GOT NO IDEA, St. CLAIR.

CLICK

YOU REALLY THINK I'M TELLING *YOU?*

YOU'RE WORTH ©250 TO ME ALIVE OR DEAD. YEAH, I THINK IT'S JUST POSSIBLE.

YOU'RE HAVIN' A *DANGEROUS DREAM,* St. CLAIR, IF YOU THINK YOU CAN BLUFF ME.

YOU *DO* ME, YOU GET NOTHIN'! TAKE ME *IN* AND I'M OUT IN A WEEK.

KEEP MOVING.

OKAY, LAZMUSI-- HOW ABOUT A NEED FOR ARTIFICIAL LIMBS? I CAN ARRANGE THAT.
LISTEN, KID, THIS KINDA ROUTINE DON'T GET ME NOTHIN' BUT ANGRY.
YOU DON'T WANT TO GET ME ANGRY, MISS St.CLAIR.
I JUST MIGHT--
LAZMUSI--
K-BLAM!
HUUAAGH!
DAMN!
I GOT TO LAZMUSI AHEAD OF STRAVIN, BUT LOOKS LIKE NOT BY ENOUGH.
POW!
ZIKE!?
10

WE MADE THE HIT. I AIN'T STICKIN' AROUND FOR THIS.
LEAVING SO SOON? I WON'T HEAR OF IT.
VROOOOOOOOM!
X-12 EXPLOSIVE PROJECTILE. I SPENT MOST OF MY LAST BOUNTY LICENSING THIS THING.
SHIN-CHUNK
KA-BWAM!
GUESS IT WAS WORTH IT.

:cough: NOT BAD, St. CLAIR. YOU GOT POTENTIAL.
LAZMUSI!?!

YEAH. :cough: HE WAS A COUPLE INCHES HIGH. STUPID BASTARDS COULDN'T DO ANYTHING RIGHT...
I NEVER WOULDA TOLD YOU A THING.

BUT NOW...?
YOU KIDDIN' ME? TWO DAYS. HE MEETS THE P.U.A. IN PARKEN SQUARE. THE TANKER LEVELS.
HELP ME UP.

GET THAT LITTLE PRIV, St. CLAIR.
NO FEAR, LAZMUSI.
GREAT KID. :cough: YOU MADE MY DAY.

SEE YA AROUND.
WHERE ARE YOU GOING? YOU NEED--
YEAH, THANKS, GRANDMA. I'LL TAKE CARE OF IT.
HELL. AND I THOUGHT ALL MUTANTS HAD BEEN OUTLAWED...

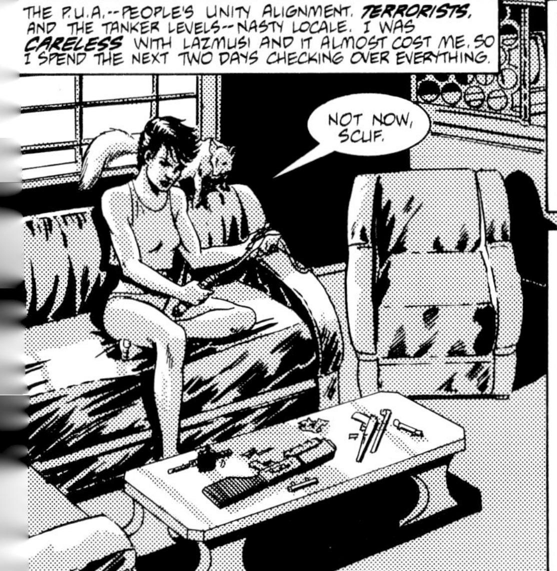
THE P.U.A.--PEOPLE'S UNITY ALIGNMENT. TERRORISTS. AND THE TANKER LEVELS--NASTY LOCALE. I WAS CARELESS WITH LAZMUSI AND IT ALMOST COST ME. SO I SPEND THE NEXT TWO DAYS CHECKING OVER EVERYTHING.
NOT NOW, SCUF.

DOXES ARE SUPPOSED TO SLOW DOWN AT YOUR AGE.
MERCY? HEY, MERCY!?
12

COME ON, LADY--WE'RE EATING OUT TODAY.
JUST LET YOURSELF IN, MOLLY.
WE ARE?

ABSOLUTELY. LUNCH AT BAYVEE'S. MY TREAT.
GIVE ME FIVE MINUTES.
BAYVEE'S IS PACKED. EVERYONE HAS COME TO TRY OUT **STRIBBERS**, THE GOVERNMENT'S NEWEST "MIRACLE FOOD" FROM SOME GENETIFARMS ON MONRO ISLAND.
THEY TASTE EXACTLY AS ONE WOULD EXPECT.
...AND I DON'T THINK PAUL WANTS TO TAKE NO FOR AN ANSWER.
GOOD FOR HIM! I ***LIKE*** PAUL.
NEW SUBJECT, MOLLY.
Bayvee's
OKAY. WHO ARE YOU AFTER THIS TIME?
SOME SMUGGLER. A GUY NAMED STRAVIN. ©20,000 WHEN I GET HIM.
20,000. WOW. HE MUST BE ***DANGEROUS***. WHAT'D HE SMUGGLE?
DON'T KNOW YET.
GOD, ARE WE SUPPOSED TO BE ***ENJOYING*** THIS STUFF?
SO YOU DON'T KNOW WHAT THIS GUY'S ACTUALLY DONE?
I KNOW THEY'VE POSTED ©20,000. DEAD OR ALIVE.
THAT'S ENOUGH FOR ME.

THEN YOU'RE JUST TRUSTING THAT THE COUNCIL HAS A GOOD REASON FOR--
I DON'T JUST TRUST *ANYONE*, MOLLY.
WELL, YOU SEEM TO TRUST THEIR *WANTED POSTERS* WHEN THEY SAY SOMEONE DESERVES TO *DIE*. "DEAD OR ALIVE," RIGHT?

WHAT DO YOU WANT ME TO DO?! I'M NOT HERE TO RUN A *CHARACTER ANALYSIS* ON EVERY SLIME THEY POST!
THEY SAY WHO THEY WANT AND I BRING 'EM IN. IT MAY NOT BE A *PERFECT* SYSTEM, BUT IF YOU ASK ME, IT'S WORKING PRETTY WELL SO FAR.

ANTARI APTS
I'M NOT SAYING IT ISN'T, MERCY. YOU'RE *GREAT* AT YOUR JOB. I KNOW THAT. I GUESS I'M JUST WONDERING IF SOMETIMES WE AREN'T LETTING THAT SYSTEM RUN US.

SPEAKING OF WHICH, I'M DUE BACK AT THE SHOP. LISTEN, JUST TAKE CARE, MERCY.
SEE YOU SOON.

14

THE TANKER LEVELS OF PARKEN SQUARE HAVE BEEN ABANDONED FOR THIRTY YEARS. THE OLD DISTILLATE LINES LOCKED THEM UP WHEN THEY WENT BUST. BUT ITS HUGE TANKS AND MAZE-LIKE SHAFTS ARE A PERFECT PLACE FOR A HUNTED MAN TO LOSE HIMSELF IN, AND THE GATES AND SEALED VENT TUBES ARE NO OBSTACLES. STRAVIN'S NOT THE FIRST MAN TO CRACK THEM.
FLIK
GOD ONLY KNOWS IF ANYONE'S GOT A MAP OF THIS PLACE. I HOPE I BROUGHT ENOUGH FLARES.
THIS WILL ONLY GET IN THE WAY DOWN THERE.
BUT THESE I'LL NEED.
I HAVE TO BE READY EVERY SECOND. IT'S NOT LIKELY I'LL BE ABLE TO SNEAK UP ON THEM.

FFTT
WHIVVVVVVVVV
USING THE REELER, I TRAVEL FOR **HOURS**. I HAVE TO RELY ON MY SENSE OF DIRECTION TO GUIDE ME DEEPER INTO THE LINES, KNOWING THAT'S WHERE STRAVIN WILL BE.
FINALLY, I HEAR FAINT VOICES, ECHOING DECEPTIVELY. I MAKE FOR THEM AS BEST AS I CAN JUDGE.
THE VOICES GROW **LOUDER** AND I KNOW I'M GETTING CLOSE.
WHEN THEY **STOP**, I'LL KNOW I'M **THERE**...
...AND THAT STRAVIN AND HIS P.U.A. PALS KNOW IT, TOO.
16

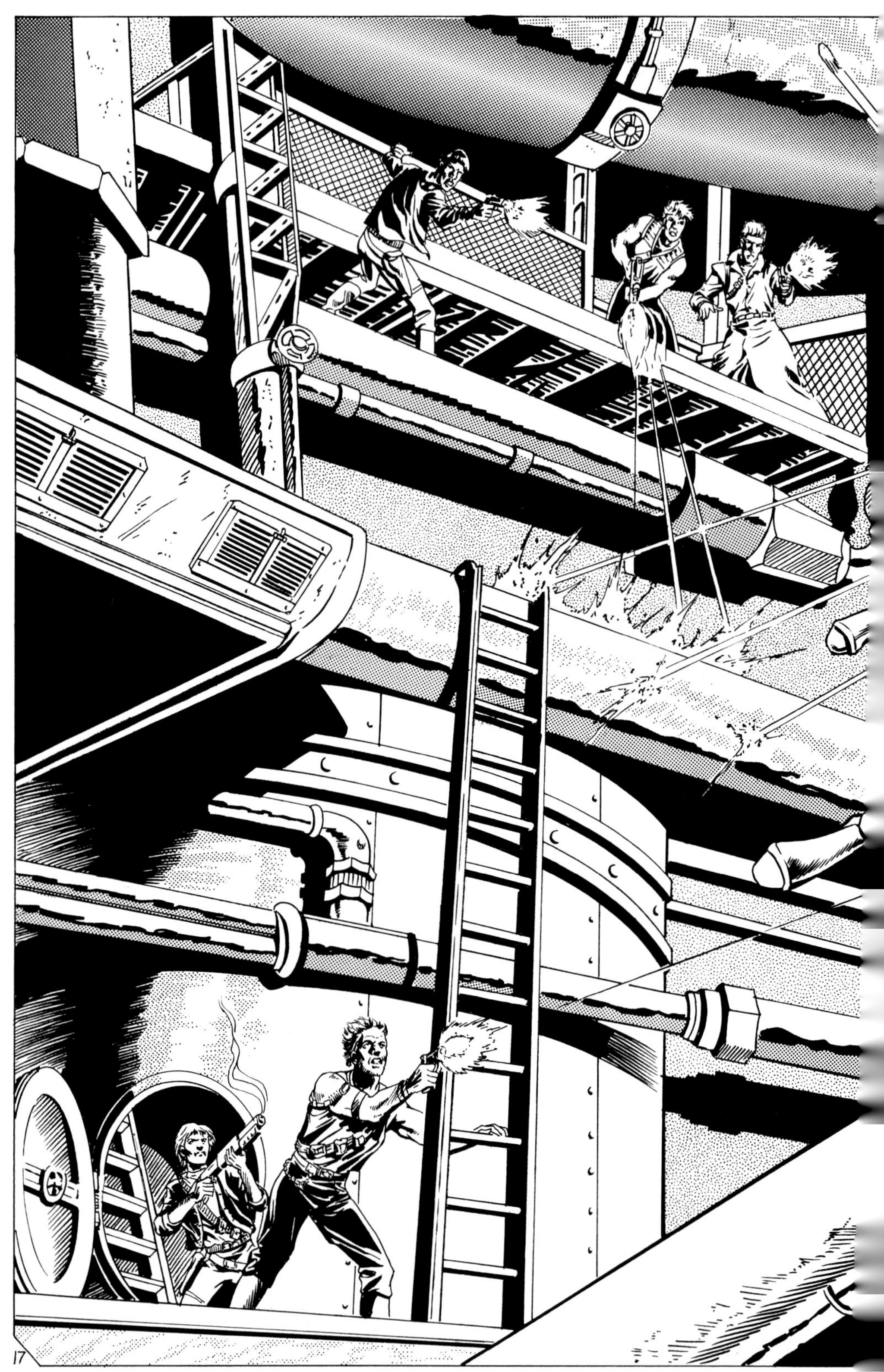
17

18

BLAMBLAMBLAM
THANK GOD THEY DON'T HAVE INFRAREDS.
THE THREE ON THE GRATING HAVE LEFT THEMSELVES WIDE OPEN.

THESE TWO HAD A BAD ANGLE TO WORK FROM.
FOOM FOOM

SO MUCH FOR THE AMATEURS. THE OTHER TWO KNOW WHAT THEY'RE DOING.

WELL, I DON'T NEED THESE FLARES ANYMORE...

CLANG
FSSSSK

BLAM BLAM
AAAAGH!

WHICH JUST LEAVES THE ONE ABOVE.
SPLANG SPAK SPAK
THAT'LL BE STRAVIN.

THAP THAP THAP
AND IT SOUNDS LIKE HE'S RUN OUT OF FIGHT.
FFFTT
SIDE PASSAGE. PERFECT SPOT FOR...
THAP THAP THAP
KPOW
HAUGH!
BLAM
20

UNNGH
CLACK
CLANG
SPLANG
BLAM
GIVE IT UP, STRAVIN, IT'S OVER.

COME OUT OF THERE...

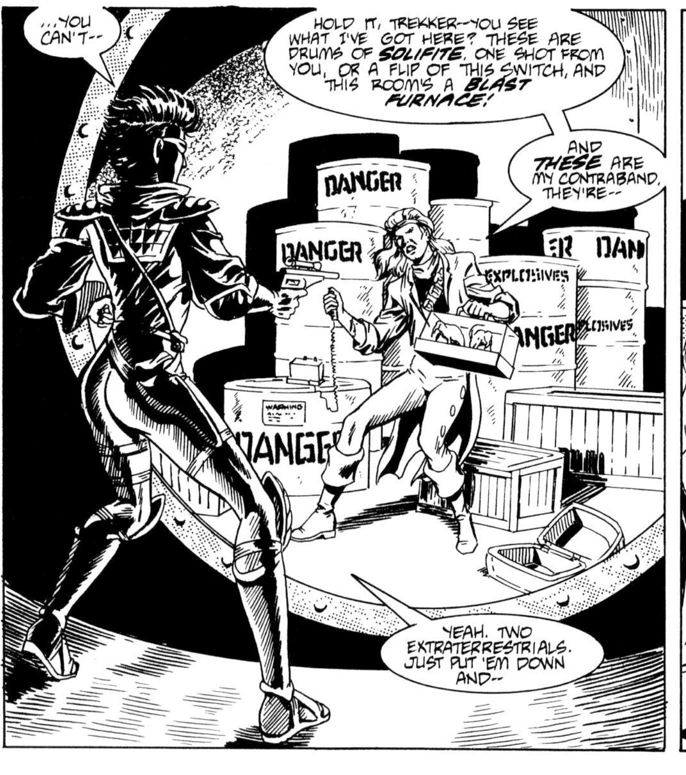
...YOU CAN'T--
HOLD IT, TREKKER--YOU SEE WHAT I'VE GOT HERE? THESE ARE DRUMS OF SOLIFITE. ONE SHOT FROM YOU, OR A FLIP OF THIS SWITCH, AND THIS ROOM'S A BLAST FURNACE!
AND THESE ARE MY CONTRABAND, THEY'RE--
DANGER
DANGER
EXPLOSIVES
DANGER
WARNING
DANGER
YEAH. TWO EXTRATERRESTRIALS. JUST PUT 'EM DOWN AND--

WHAT DO YOU SUPPOSE THEY THREATEN THIS DIRTBALL WORLD WITH, TREKKER? DISEASE? RADIATION? NO.
FOOD. FREE FOOD.

THESE ARE QUILLONS. THEY EAT ANYTHING, BREED LIKE CRAZY, AND THEY'RE A NEAR-PERFECT FOOD SOURCE FOR MAN, BUT--GUESS WHAT? THESE ARE THE LAST TWO ALIVE.
THAT'S BECAUSE YOUR GOVERNMENT WIPED 'EM OFF THE FACE OF DIONET SO WE COULDN'T GET THEM TO THE P.U.A.
THAT'S CRAZY, STRAVIN. PUT DOWN THAT DETONATOR. YOU WON'T GAIN ANYTHING BY--
I WON'T LET THE COUNCIL GET THEM. THE QUILLONS MEAN ECONOMIC CONTROL HERE. YOUR FASCIST REGIME KNOWS THAT.

YOU HAVE TO LET ME GO! THE P.U.A. WILL USE THESE QUILLONS TO LIBERATE THE PEOPLE.
LET YOU GO? YOU'VE JUST BEEN TRYING TO KILL ME, YOU STUPID--

WE DO WHAT WE HAVE TO! DON'T YOU KNOW WHAT IT IS TO WORK FOR A CAUSE GREATER THAN YOURSELF?
BUT NO, I CAN SEE YOU DON'T. THIS IS USELESS.
STRAVIN-- DON'T...

FOR THE PEOPLE.
CLICK
FA-THOOOM
22

THERE ISN'T ENOUGH LEFT OF THE BODY FOR AN I.D., SO I CAN'T CLAIM THE ©20,000. FORTUNATELY, SOME OF THE P.U.A. ARE WANTED, SO AT LEAST I WON'T STARVE TO DEATH THIS MONTH.
I DON'T TELL ANYONE ABOUT THE QUILLONS, OF COURSE. STRAVIN'S STORY IS EITHER CRAZY, OR IT'S DANGEROUS INFORMATION. EITHER WAY, IT'S NOT THE KIND OF NEWS YOU SPREAD AROUND.

I DO TELL MOLLY, THOUGH. FOR SOME REASON, I TELL HER.
...CAN'T BELIEVE STRAVIN KILLING HIMSELF. WHAT A FANATIC.
WHAT WAS IT HE SAID? "A CAUSE GREATER THAN YOURSELF..?"

SOUNDS LIKE HE WAS VERY DESPERATE TO ME, YOU KNOW, "DESPERATE TIMES, DESPERATE PEOPLE..."
LOTS OF PEOPLE ARE DESPERATE. BUT YO JUST DON'T GO OFF MURDERING AND TERRORIZING. THIS IS A CIVILIZED SOCIETY. THERE AR SYSTEMS HERE.

AND IF THOSE SYSTEMS DON'T WORK FOR SOMEONE ...?
THEN TOUGH. THAT'S JUST THE BREAKS...
sigh I DON'T KNO I'M JUST TIRED.

I WAKE UP AT DAWN THE NEXT MORNING. THE SKY GLOWS RED WITH THE RISING SUN. IT BLUSHES THE STREETS, THE CARS, AND THE BUILDINGS RED. COLOR OF PASSION. OF PURPOSE. OF LIFE. BLOOD RED.

I GATHER MY GEAR. BY THE TIME I LEAVE, THE SUN WILL HAVE CLIMBED INTO THE THICK HAZE AND THE COLOR WILL HAVE DRAINED. I'LL WALK OUT ONCE AGAIN INTO THE GRAY AND AIMLESS STREETS OF NEW GELAPH.

THE TRAIL TO SCARMEN'S BURN

Story and art
RON RANDALL

Lettering
KEN BRUZENAK

Chapter break art
RON RANDALL WITH STEVE MATTSSON

History repeatedly shows us that man is basically a social creature. The drive to community has shaped our world. Our greatest achievements are measured by their impact on our civilization.
History is also filled, however, with stories of those who shun, despise, and even assault the very societies into which they are born. This has been Man's conflict through the ages...
ALL THAT'S FROM A PAPER I'M WORKING ON.

OF COURSE, YOU NEEDN'T TURN TO THE LESSONS OF HISTORY TO FEEL THESE PARADOXICAL URGES MADE MANIFEST. NOT, AT LEAST, IF YOU LIVE AS I DO IN THE MAZE OF ANTARI ALLEY, IN NEW GELAPH, IN THE YEAR 2226.
DOWN IN THESE CRUMBLING BLOCKS, YOU CONSTANTLY FACE THE WORST PRODUCTS OF OUR GRAND SOCIETY-- THE POVERTY, THE GREED, THE VIOLENCE.

ON THE OTHER HAND, THERE'S A CERTAIN EDGE TO THE PEOPLE LIVING HERE--A CHALLENGING ALERTNESS. A FASCINATING SPARK WHICH CAN MAKE FOR MUCH STIMULATING INTERACTION.
FOR EXAMPLE, THERE'S THIS ONE YOUNG WOMAN ON MY FLOOR...
DAMN!
COME ON, YOU...
ANTARI APTS

The Trail to Scarmen's Burn
DAMN!
BASH
DAMN!
BASH
DAMN!
BASH
UH... THE TUBES ARE OUT, MERCY. I HEAR THEY'LL BE WORKING ON THEM TOMORROW.
MERCY St. CLAIR IS A TREKKER-- A (RELUCTANTLY) GOVERNMENT-SANCTIONED BOUNTY HUNTER.
I GUESS ANOTHER LESSON FROM HISTORY IS THAT HUMAN SOCIETIES OFTEN PRODUCE A GREATER CRIMINAL ELEMENT THAN THEIR POLICING FORCES CAN HANDLE BY THEMSELVES...
created, written & drawn by RON RANDALL
lettered by KEN BRUZENAK
2

WELL, THAT'S GREAT, ISN'T IT, THOM? THIS IS THE THIRD TIME THIS MONTH!

YOU ON A TRAIL NOW, MERCY?
JUST BARELY. THERE'S A BIG PRICE ON SOME MANIAC WHO ROBBED A BANK, KILLED FIFTEEN OR SO HOSTAGES, AND ESCAPED INTO THE WASTELANDS.
2
STAIRS

MY CHANCES OF TRACKING HIM OUT THERE ARE SLIM--AND GETTING WORSE EVERY MINUTE. I'VE GOT TO--
3

WAIT A MINUTE--HE MUST BE :puff: HEADING FOR THIS SCARMEN'S BURN THEN, RIGHT?
YEAH, THAT'S THE THEORY...
...IF THERE EVEN IS A SCARMEN'S BURN.

THEN HOLD UP! :puff: I THINK I CAN HELP YOU OUT! COME ON IN TO MY PLACE.
WHAT? ARE YOU CRAZY?

ONLY TAKE YOU A MINUTE TO FIND OUT.

HIS IS ALMOST TOO GOOD TO BE TRUE. FOR MONTHS I'VE BEEN TRYING TO FIGURE OUT HOW TO MAKE AN **MPRESSION** ON THIS WOMAN. NOW I HAVE A GOLDEN OPPORTUNITY. I PUT ON MY BEST PROFESSIONAL IR-- I DON'T PLAN TO BLOW THIS CHANCE.

HAVE A SEAT, MERCY. JUST GIVE ME A SECOND AND I'LL SHOW YOU SOME MATERIAL THAT COULD GIVE YOU THAT BOUNTY ON A PLATTER.
YOU, UH, WORKING ON ANOTHER **PAPER**, BY ANY CHANCE, THOM?

OF COURSE, ERCY. THOMPSON ICHARDS KNOWS NO REST.

HOW ELSE S A "RELEASED" ISTORY PROF GOING TO EAT?

NOW THEN, AS YOU KNOW, THE POPULAR RUMOR-- AND STANDARD POLICE WISDOM--HAS IT THAT "SCARMEN'S BURN" REFERS TO THE DECISIVE VICTORY OF ***COL. TRAGE SCARMAN*** IN THE WAR OF THE--

LOOK, THOMPSON, I DON'T HAVE TIME FOR A HISTORY LESSON.

RIGHT. SORRY. HERE'S THE POINT: THAT BATTLE RAGED OVER A HUGE, REMOTE AREA, NEARLY 150 YEARS AGO...

"WHEN THE COPS FIRST HEARD HINTS OF THIS OUTLAWS' HAVEN, THEY SEARCHED FOR ***MONTHS*** LOOKING FOR A TRACE OF IT.

"FINALLY THEY GAVE UP-- TOO HARD ON THE CITY'S BUDGET."

THOM, I ***KNOW*** ALL THIS. I HAVE TO GET MOVING. I--

THEY WERE LOOKING IN THE WRONG PLACE.

WHAT?

4

THEY WERE OFF BY A COUPLE OF HUNDRED MILES. LOOK--THIS BOOK IS AN OBSCURE HISTORY OF THE OUTLAWS WHO THRIVED AMONG THE BORDERS DURING THE FLARE-UPS OF THE MID-21st CENTURY.
LOOK AT THIS ENTRY...
"IT'S A BALLAD OF ONE LITTLE-KNOWN WASTELANDER WHO, AFTER SEVERAL COLORFUL EXPLOITS, STOLE A LINER AND MADE FOR THE TERRITORIES.
"HE ELUDED HIS PURSUERS, BUT THE LINER WAS CRIPPLED. IT APPARENTLY CRASHED IN THE WASTES...
"...CRASHED AND BURNED."
THE OUTLAW'S NAME WAS SCARMEN.
LINERS
SCARMEN'S BURN.
EXACTLY. AND YOU SEE, NO ONE REMEMBERS THIS SCARMEN. IF I HADN'T STUMBLED ACROSS THIS OLD VOLUME--
WHY HAVEN'T YOU TAKEN THIS TO THE COPS?
I DID! AS SOON AS I FOUND THIS BOOK.
I COULD USE THAT MONEY THEY'RE OFFERING FOR A LEAD TO THE BURN.
BUT THEIR DAMN COMPUTER CHECK CAM UP EMPTY AN THEY SENT M PACKING. IT W JUST ANOTHER CRACKPOT THEORY TO THEM.

SO I'VE BEEN RESEARCHING CROSS-REFERENCES TO--
"CROSS-REFERENCES"!? WHAT IS THIS, A DAMNED TERM PAPER?
THAT'S WHAT THE POLICE SAY THEY NEED TO WARRANT THE EXPENSE OF A SEARCH.

WELL, I DON'T NEED A TEXTBOOK ENTRY! WHERE DOES THIS BOOK SAY HE CRASHED? I'LL BRING YOU YOUR "CROSS-REFERENCES."
WHAT.. ALONE? I DON'T KNOW, MERCY. SHOULDN'T YOU WAIT AND ROUND UP SOME--

I TOLD YOU, THOM-- THERE'S NO TIME. HE GETS CLOSER TO THE BURN EVERY SECOND. IF HE REACHES IT, I LOSE. HE'LL BE UNTOUCHABLE.
PLEASE, THOMPSON, I NEED THIS BREAK!

AS I SAID, LIVING HERE CAN MAKE FOR SOME STIMULATING INTERACTIONS.
OKAY, MERCY. IF THAT'S WHAT YOU WANT.

THE BOOK PROVIDES A SKETCHY DESCRIPTION OF THE CRASH AREA. THE FIRST REFERENCE IT MAKES IS TO THE PLACE CALLED "NEEDLE ROCK."
AND THIS IS A MAP OF THE TERRAIN AT THE CRASH SITE. PROBABLY MADE BY SOME DISAPPOINTED TREASURE HUNTER.
6

IF YOU CAN FIND THAT "NEEDLE ROCK," YOU SHOULD BE IN BUSINESS.
IT'LL HAVE TO DO. NOW I JUST NEED TO BORROW SOMEBODY'S...
I KNOW...
...SOMEONE'S CAR.
THANKS, THOM. WE'LL BE SPLITTING THAT REWARD IN A WEEK!
UH, MERCY...?
MAYBE I SHOULD GO WITH YOU.
HA, HA! SEE YOU SOON, THOM.
KLIK
WELL, SO MUCH FOR MY "STRONG IMPRESSION..."
...WHAT DOES MERCY THINK I AM? THE WASTELANDS CAN'T BE THAT TOUGH...
TRADE &

W-WELCOME TO BEN'S TRADE AND FUEL. WHAT CAN I GET YA, MISTER?

JUST THE TWO OF YOU HERE? AND THE GIRL?
UH, WELL, YEAH--FER NOW--BUT FOLKS IS ALWAYS COMIN' IN FOR FILL-UPS. SEE, WE'RE 'BOUT A TANKFUL OUTTA NEW GELAPH... AND...

...THEY COULD BE SWARMIN' IN ANY MINUTE...

SHE'S WASTING HER TIME.

"WE DON'T KNOW WHERE HE IS OR WHAT HE'S DOING. HE COULD BE KILLING AGAIN RIGHT NOW...
"...AND YOU'RE TELLING ME TO CALL IN THE SEARCH?!"

YES, I KNOW ABOUT THE FUNDING SHORTAGE, I KNOW OUR RESOURCES ARE...YES, BUT HILTS IS A WALKING SLAUGHTERHOUSE!

I DON'T CARE HOW MUCH IT COSTS, WE--OF COURSE NOT, CHIEF, I--NO, NO, ALL RIGHT.

I UNDERSTAND. YOU'LL KEEP IT HIGH ON YOUR LIST OF PRIORITIES.

YES, CHIEF.

BRING THEM IN, LANGSTROM. ALL OF THEM.
YES, LIEUTENANT.
LT. ALEX ST. CLAIR

IT'S NOT EASY LETTING ONE LIKE HILTS GO. SO, ONCE AGAIN, I FALL INTO A HABIT THIS JOB HAS TAUGHT ME SO WELL... I CLUTCH AT A STRAW...
...MAYBE SOME TREKKER WILL GET LUCKY AND DRAG HIM IN. MAYBE IT'LL EVEN BE MY NIECE, MERCY...

SIX HOURS OUT OF THE CITY, I'M REACHING THE END OF MY FUEL AND THE EDGE OF TRAVELED TERRAIN. STANDARD MAPS GET VAGUE FROM HERE ON.
BUT THEY DO SHOW ONE LAST FUEL-UP POST ALONG THE COURSE SUGGESTED IN THOMPSON'S BOOK.
WHETHER IT IS THE RIGHT COURSE IS ANOTHER QUESTION.
SO IS MY FINDING THAT "NEEDLE ROCK."
I TRY NOT TO THINK ABOUT THE ODDS ON THOSE QUESTIONS.
THE FUEL-UP SHOULD BE JUST--
UH-OH.
DAMN.
HE'S BEEN HERE, ALL RIGHT.

LOOKS LIKE HE TOOK WHAT SUPPLIES AND FUEL HE COULD CARRY AND TORCHED THE REST--INCLUDING THESE THREE POOR SOULS.
WHICH MAKES CATCHING HIM THAT MUCH MORE URGENT--AND THAT MUCH MORE IMPOSSIBLE. THIS IS A BIG LAND TO TACKLE WITH AN EMPTY FUEL TANK.
SO, WHAT'S YOUR NEXT MOVE NOW, TREKKER?
WHAT--
WHIIIIIZZZZZ
SPAK
SPLANG
KRAK
BEEOW
TUNG
CHUD
SPANG
SPANG
BLAP
SPANG

LOOKS LIKE WE GOT 'ER, RAMSEY.
"LOOKS LIKE"?! GET YOUR BUTT DOWN THERE AND FIND OUT!
I'M GETTIN' TIRED OF HIM.
YEAH. RAMSEY'S SUCH A JUMPY LITTLE PRIN WHENEVER HE LEAVES THE BURN.
WHERE THE HELL IS SHE? SHE COULDN'T HAVE MADE IT OUT OF OUR FIRE, COULD SHE?
NO WAY. NOT UNLESS SHE WAS A DAMN GOOD MAGICIAN.
OR MAYBE A TREKKER?
A TREKKER? AW, HELL.
CARE TO DROP THE WEAPONS?
TAKE HER DOWNNNNGH!
BLAM BLAM
KPOW
THEY NEVER CARE TO DROP THEIR WEAPONS.
THE OTHER CAR'LL BE CIRCLING ROUND BACK BY NOW.
12

YUP, AND AT A FAIR DISTANCE, TOO.
GUESS THEY FIGURE I DON'T KNOW HOW TO USE THIS PEASHOOTER.
KRAK
KRAK
IT TAKES ABOUT TWENTY MINUTES TO LOAD UP THE FASTEST OF THEIR RIGS. THESE SOUPED-UP DESERT ROVERS ARE MUCH FASTER THAN ANYTHING CITY LEGAL, EVEN THE POLICE VAN HILTS STOLE.
THEIR DESERT-READY GEAR WILL COME IN HANDY, TOO. A FAIR EXCHANGE FOR A LITTLE FLESH WOUND.
I'LL PICK UP THE FOUR DUSTERS ON MY WAY OUT. I DON'T RECOGNIZE ANY OF THEM, BUT THEY MAY BE WORTH SOMETHING. THOM'S CAR'LL WAIT, TOO.
TWO HOURS LATER, I'VE GOT TO BE RUNNING ON FUMES, AND NO SIGN OF HILTS. I MAKE FOR THE TALLEST MESA I CAN SEE, AND BREAK OUT THE DUSTERS' BINOCULARS.

THE VIEW'S WORTH THE CLIMB. THE LENS CUTS THROUGH THE DESERT HAZE. I'M LOOKING STRAIGHT AT ONE VERY ENCOURAGING IMAGE...
...THAT LOOKS FOR ALL THE WORLD LIKE A NEEDLE ROCK TO ME.
AND THERE'S SOMETHING AT ITS BASE...
...SOMETHING MOVING. I HIT THE RANGE ADJUST.
S OUT OF RANGE FOR A SHOT, BUT WON'T TAKE LONG TO CLOSE THE STANCE.
THE PASS HE USED IS TIGHT. IF HE SPOTTED ME, WHICH I DOUBT, IT'D BE THE PLACE FOR AN AMBUSH.
KEEP MY EYES N THE ROCKS, UST IN CASE.
A GUY LIKE HILTS CAN BE FULL OF SURPRISES.
14

KERWHAAAAM
CAN'T...
...LET...
...HIM...
BLAM
BLAM

SPAK
SPAK SPAK
DAMN CHICK'S TOUGHER'N SHE LOOKS.
WELL, YA GAVE 'ER A GAME TRY, BABE, BUT--
GONE. SHE MUSTA DRAGGED HER BONES INTO THE BRUSH.
GOOD EFFORT, TREKKER! MAYBE YOU FIGURE I'LL JUST LEAVE YOU IN THERE?
NO WAY. NOT ME. THAT'S BEIN' SLOPPY. I LIKE TA FINISH WHAT'S STARTED.
MAYBE YOU'VE NOTICED.
DON'T BLACK OUT... DON'T...
I'M COMIN' IN FOR YA, BABE. GONNA GET TO KNOW YA...
GOTTA KEEP MOVING... NIGHT SOON... SAFER THEN...
...KNOW YA REAL WELL...
CAN'T GO INTO SHOCK...
...THEN I'M GONNA KILL YA.
HEAR ME, TREKKER?
"IS MERCY THERE...?"
16

NO, PAUL. NO. SHE'S NOT HERE. IN FACT, I HAVEN'T SEEN HER MUCH RECENTLY. COME ON IN.
THANKS, MOLLY. I THOUGHT WE HAD A DATE FOR TONIGHT, BUT SHE WASN'T AT HER PLACE.
GUESS SOMETHING CAME UP. YOU KNOW MERCY.
UH-HUH. SOMETHING'S ALWAYS COMING UP WITH HER!
SHE'S A HARD WOMAN TO PIN DOWN, THAT'S FOR SURE.
IN MORE WAYS THAN ONE, RIGHT?
OH, YOU HEARD, THEN. YEAH, MERCY'S NOT EXACTLY RUSHING OUR RELATIONSHIP ALONG.
I WAS HOPING TO ENTICE HER--I'VE GOT TO GO OFF PLANET FOR A FEW DAYS. THOUGHT I'D TRY TO TALK HER INTO COMING ALONG.
I WANT TO GET HER OUT OF THIS TOWN FOR A WHILE--GIVE HER A CHANCE TO BREATHE EASY. MAYBE THEN... WELL...
HANG IN THERE, PAUL. MERCY REALLY IS A SWEET PERSON. SHE JUST DOESN'T KNOW IT YET.
YEAH, SHE'S TOO BUSY "TAMING THE STREETS" SINGLE-HANDEDLY.
I DON'T KNOW, MOLLY...

"MERCY ALWAYS SEEMS TO BE IN OVER HER HEAD."
SHE'S MADE IT FARTHER THAN I'D EXPECTED. MUSTA HAD SOME QUAVINE PILLS OR SOMETHIN' TO KEEP HER GOIN' AFTER THE CRASH, BUT THERE'S ENOUGH MOON TO FOLLOW HER TRACK.
AND I HAD TO FOLLOW HER. SHE'S THE TYPE WON'T GIVE UP. JUST KEEP HOUNDIN' YA...
...HOUNDIN YA TO DEATH.
OKAY. BUT IT WON'T BE MY DEATH.
SHAK
SHAK
BLAM
BRAKABRAK
18

JUST MAKING IT TO THE MARSHES NEARLY *FINISHED* ME. SO I HAVE TO END THIS *FAST*.

ONLY PROBLEM IS I HAD TO KEEP MY RIFLE DRY...

HUNNNG

VERY GOOD, BABE. ONE GOOD ROPE TRICK DESERVES ANOTHER, HUH? WELL-- THIS WAS NOTHIN' *PERSONAL*, YA KNOW...
...UNTIL NOW.

WHUHH
WHUD

WHACK

I'M THROUGH DANCIN' WITH YA, LADY. YOU NEVER SHOULDA LEFT YOUR NICE LITTLE CITY.
NEVER SHOULDA GOT ME MAD...
SHIK-CHUNK
WE COULDA HAD A GREAT TIME TOGETH--
SPLOOP
--AUUUUH?!
MY GOD--I WAS DOWN THERE, WITH THAT?
WHATEVER IT IS, IT DRAGS HILTS OUT INTO THE DEEPER WATERS. AFTER A MINUTE, BLOOD COMES BUBBLING TO THE SURFACE...
...BUT IT'S NOT HILTS'S! THEN I HEAR HIM, SLOSHING AWAY IN THE MURKY DISTANCE. THE HUNT ISN'T OVER YET.
20

I TAKE MY LAST TWO QUAVINE PILLS, GRAB MY GEAR, AND BREAK OUT THE REELER. NO WAY I'M GOING TO GO WADING HERE AFTER SEEING THAT CREATURE.
FFFT
I MEAN, WHAT IF THAT ONE WAS A BABY?
WITH THE INFRAREDS, IT DOESN'T TAKE LONG TO PICK UP HIS TRAIL. BY DAWN, THE TREES GIVE WAY TO MORE BROKEN COUNTRY.
MY LEGS SAY STOP. I IGNORE THEM.
BY MIDDAY, I'M GETTING CLOSE TO THE BURN, ACCORDING TO THOMPSON'S BOOK.
HILTS'S TRACKS LEAD DOWN INTO A THICK TANGLE OF TREES, HEADING STRAIGHT FOR A PASS BEYOND. BUT THE MAP I HAVE SAYS FOLLOWING THIS RIDGE WILL GET ME THERE, TOO. IF SO, IT'LL BE MUCH QUICKER TRAVELING.
MAKES ME GLAD I'VE LUGGED THE DAMN BOOK ALONG.
GREVI! YOU MADE IT--AT LAST!

IT'S BEEN A LONG TIME, BABY. THOUGHT I'D SURPRISE YOU.
CANTEEN AND A GUN.
IN THE SHIP. WHY? WHAT'S WRONG?
THERE'S SOME CRAZY TREKKER ON MY TAIL, WE HAVE TO--
KA-BLAM!
DID I HEAR THE LADY SAY THERE'S A CANTEEN IN THE SHIP? I COULD KILL FOR A DRINK RIGHT NOW.
BACK AWAY FROM THE SHIP, HILTS.
MY BODY FEELS
EADY TO CAVE
N AFTER THE
UN. BUT I
AN'T SHOW THAT
O THESE TWO.
IT'S OVER. ON THE GROUND. HANDS BEHIND YOUR HEADS.
DROP THE PIECE, BABE, OR I'LL DO HER, I SWEAR!
GREVI?!?
YOU'RE KIDDING, RIGHT? YOUR FRIEND'S SILLCA BLAIN, ISN'T SHE? TWO COUNTS OF MURDER, FIVE ARMED ROBBERIES, AND ARSON.
NOT MUCH OF A HOSTAGE, HILTS.
I'M A TREKKER, REMEMBER?
22

AND THIS GUN WILL SHOOT THROUGH TWO BODIES AS EASILY AS ONE.
RIGHT. IN MY DREAMS, MAYBE...
...BUT HILTS DOESN'T KNOW THAT.
GUESS I DON'T HAVE MUCH CHOICE THEN...
GREVI...?
SORRY, SILLCA!
OOF!
WHAT--?
BLAM
NO!

HILTS-- YOU BASTARD!

BLAM
COUGH!

I DON'T KNOW WHY I STOP FOR BLAIN. THERE'S LITTLE I CAN DO.

THEN I LURCH OFF AGAIN. HILTS HASN'T GAINED MUCH TIME AND HIS TRAIL'S STILL EASY TO FOLLOW.
SOON HIS SIGNS TURN UP A STEEP CLIFF. GOD--AFTER ALL THIS, HE WANTS TO CLIMB?
THE SCRAMBLE UP TAKES AN ETERNITY. MY HEAD SWIMS-- MY EYES DON'T WANT TO FOCUS ON THE CRUMBLING ROCKS I CLAW INTO.
I FEEL LIKE I'M MOVING IN SLOW MOTION.
BUT NEAR THE TOP, I CATCH A DISTANT GLIMMER--SUNLIGHT ON METAL.
SCARMEN'S BURN. SAFETY FOR HILTS IF I LET HIM REACH IT.
MY ARMS THROB THEIR PROTESTS AS I FRANTICALLY HAUL MYSELF UP THE LAST OUTCROP. I HAVE TO CATCH HILTS NOW--
--MY TIME'S UP.
24

TREKKER--!
END OF THE ROAD.
AGGGH!
FFFT
RANDALL '87

BY THE TIME SHE STOPS ROLLING, I'LL BE BACK AT THE SHIP.
SILLCA SAID THERE WAS A GUN INSIDE. ONCE I GET IT, I'LL...
BLOOD.
HOW DID...
26

BOOM!!!
SILLCA...HOW... *COUGH*...DID YOU EVEN GET...UP THERE...?
NO MYSTERY, HILTS...
...I HELPED HER.
SOMEHOW I MANAGED TO HAUL HILTS'S CORPSE INTO THE CRUISER. IT'LL BE A LONG TRIP BACK WITH TWO BODIES FOR COMPANY.
SHE TOLD ME SHE WOULDN'T KILL HIM. MAYBE SHE LIED TO ME. MAYBE, IN DYING, HER AIM WAS OFF. EITHER WAY, IT FEELS LIKE HILTS GOT THE KIND OF JUSTICE YOU'D EXPECT OUT HERE, BRUTAL, STARK, AND FINAL.
BACK IN THE CITY, THOMPSON WILL BE GLAD HIS BOOK IS RIGHT. I'LL BE GLAD JUST TO GET HOME. EVEN WHEN HOME IS NEW GELAPH.

RULES OF THE GAME

Story and art
RON RANDALL

Lettering
KEN BRUZENAK

Chapter break art
RON RANDALL WITH DON WALLACE

BLOOD...
...SHE'S INSIDE!
BRAKKA BRAKKA
BRAKKA
CHUD
VIP
VIP
VIP
TZING
BEEOW
BRAKKA BRAKKA
N-NOOOO!

Rules of the Gam

created, written & drawn by RON RANDALL · letters by KEN BRUZENA

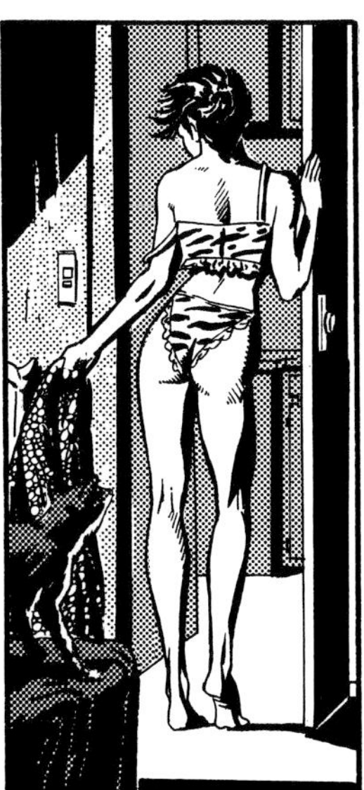

THE NIGHTMARE AGAIN. I'D THOUGHT IT WOULD HAVE ENDED BY NOW.
BUT I MADE SLIPS WITH HILTS. TOO MANY ROOKIE MISTAKES. IT COULD HAVE ENDED LIKE THAT.

WHEN YOU MAKE YOUR LIVING TRACKING DOWN BOUNTIED CRIMINALS, YOU OFTEN BRING YOUR WORK HOME WITH YOU.
THIS ISN'T THE FIRST HAZY SUNRISE THAT I'VE WATCHED FROM THIS WINDOW.

KNOCK KNOCK
OH, THAT'S RIGHT. PAUL SAID HE'D BE DROPPING BY.
3

GOOD MORNING, MERCY. I CAN'T STAY LONG. McFEARSON AND I HAVE A STAKEOUT.

MORNING, PAUL. WHAT DID YOU NEED TO TALK ABOUT?

WELL, FIRST I WANTED TO SEE HOW YOU'RE DOING. YOU LOOKED PRETTY BANGED UP WHEN YOU BROUGHT IN HILTS THE OTHER DAY.

HIYA, SCUF.

NOTHING SERIOUS. I'M FINE NOW, THANKS.

WHAT DID YOU ***REALLY*** COME FOR? YOU COULD'VE ASKED THAT ON THE PHONE.

MAYBE I JUST WANTED TO SEE YOU IN ***BEDCLOTHES*** AGAIN. IT'S BEEN A WHILE, YOU KNOW.

OKAY, OKAY!
ACTUALLY, I HAVE TO GO OFF PLANET NEXT WEEK ON ASSIGNMENT. WHEN I'M DONE, I THOUGHT I'D TAKE IN THE VENUSIAN TOUR.
FOUR PLANETS. IT'S SUPPOSED TO BE WONDERFUL.

ANYWAY, I BOUGHT TWO TICKETS. ONE OF THEM'S FOR YOU.
ARE YOU INTERESTED?

PAUL, I DON'T WANT YOU TO--
NO STRINGS. JUST A VACATION TOGETHER. WE'LL SEE HOW IT GOES.
COME ON, MERCY, WHAT DO YOU SAY?

I...I'LL LET YOU KNOW.
FAIR ENOUGH. I'LL SETTLE FOR THAT.

GOT TO RUN. YOU'LL CALL ME SOON?
SURE.

THE VENUSIAN TOUR. THEY DO SAY IT'S BEAUTIFUL.

BUT HOW DIFFERENT CAN IT REALLY BE OUT THERE?

AFTER ALL, PEOPLE ARE PEOPLE, WHETHER THEY LIVE ON THE TRILLIUS COLONIES...

...OR DOWN HERE IN THE STREETS OF NEW GELAPH...
POLICE

...IT'S THE SAME HUMAN NATURE THAT SHAPES THEIR LIVES...
POLICE
POLICE

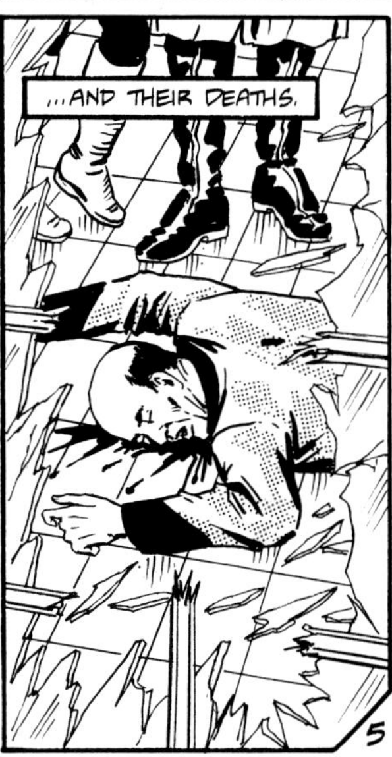
...AND THEIR DEATHS.
5

INITIAL COMP SCANS COMING IN NOW, LIEUTENANT. DOESN'T LOOK LIKE WE'RE GETTING MUCH, THOUGH.
BINGHAM, THAT'S COUNCILMAN VELANDER DOWN THERE. WHOEVER TAGGED HIM ISN'T LIKELY TO HAVE LEFT MUCH OF A CALLING CARD, IS HE?
DIG HARDER.
"VELANDER. JUST GREAT. ONE OF THE BIGGEST COGS IN NEW GELAPH'S CORRODED POLITICAL MACHINE.
"LOOKING DOWN AT HIS CORPSE, I COULD ALREADY FEEL THE INEVITABLE POLITICAL TORNADOES BEARING IN ON ME.
"FROM ONE SIDE WOULD COME THE HOWLS FOR AN EARLY CONVICTION. FROM THE OTHER, FIERCE AND INSIDIOUS EFFORTS TO THWART MY MEN'S EVERY MOVE. I SAW IT ALL COMING."
...AND I WAS RIGHT. THAT'S WHY I'VE COME TO YOU, MERCY. I NEED SOMEONE OUTSIDE THE FORCE, WHO WON'T BE HAMPERED BY THE RED TAPE THEY'LL TIE US UP IN...
...SOMEONE WHO'S GOT THE KIND OF CONTACTS MY MEN CAN'T HAVE, AND SOMEONE I CAN TRUST.
I USUALLY KNOW WHO I'M GOING AFTER, UNCLE ALEX. I'M A TREKKER, NOT A DETECTIVE.
ANTARI A
I KNOW, MERCY. BUT LISTEN--VELANDER'S CHIEF POLITICAL NEMESIS WAS COUNCILMAN GRAY, AND WE BOTH KNOW HIS CONNECTIONS TO--
--GATEFISH STRAUSS. YOU THINK HE'S BEHIND THE HIT.
COULD BE. AT LEAST IT'S A PLACE TO START.
ALL RIGH UNCLE ALE I'LL DO WHA I CAN.

THE LOOK IN MY UNCLE'S EYES TOLD ME I'D SAY YES. HE'S FIGHTING FOR HIS JOB, AND HE'S IN A NO-WIN SITUATION.
I WORK FAST, HOPING TO CATCH SOME LEADS BEFORE THE GRAPEVINE SCUTTLE-BUTT CAN BE SHUT DOWN. BUT WHOEVER MADE THE HIT HAS BEEN THOROUGH AND I'M COMING UP EMPTY.

FINALLY, I RUN INTO LAZMUSI...
St. CLAIR! YOU SHOULD ALWAYS CHECK WITH ME FIRST. I STILL OWE YOU FOR GETTING STRAVIN FOR ME.

THE VELANDER SHOOT, HUH? IT'LL BE A TOUGH NUT.
LET'S SEE NOW... POLITICAL HIT, SO THE PAYOFF'LL COME 48 HOURS OR MORE AFTER THE SHOOT. USUALLY THE MEET'S IN THE OLD ASTRO-LINE GROUNDS.

THEN THEY'LL NEED TO ET THE TRIGGER OUTTA NEW LAPH. PROBABLY OFF PLANET. AT'S WORKED OUT SEPARATELY, A FEW DAYS LATER...
LAZMUSI-- HOW DO YOU KNOW ALL THIS?

THIS IS ALL STANDARD PRACTICE, KID. YOU'RE STILL JUST A BIT WET BEHIND THE EARS ON THE FINE POINTS OF THIS RACKET, THAT'S ALL.
YOU'D BEST HAUNT THE ASTROLINE GROUNDS. MEANTIME, I'LL SEE WHAT ELSE I CAN DIG UP.

KEEP 'ER LOW TO THE GROUND, St. CLAIR.
7

HAUNTING THE SPRAWLING ASTROLINE GROUNDS IS NOT AN EASY JOB, BUT, SOMEHOW, I'M WILLING TO TRUST LAZMUSI'S LEAD-- ALMOST DESPITE MYSELF.

IF ASTROSHIPPING EVER GETS ITS ACT TOGETHER, THESE TANK TOWERS WILL BE BUSTLING AGAIN. BUT FOR NOW, THEY'RE SILENT. UNTIL...

IT'S A MEET, ALL RIGHT. AND THEY DIDN'T BRING ENOUGH PROTECTION FROM PEEPING TOMS...
FINE BY ME.

JUST HAVE TO MOVE DOWN TO WHERE I CAN USE THE REELER, AND...

WHOA!
DAMN, THA
WAS SLIC
NO NOISE N
DON'T WAN
ALERT TH
GUYS...

...ESPECIALLY SINCE THIS IS GONNA BE MY BUST.
WHUMP

SORRY FOR THE ROUGH TREATMENT, BUT I'VE GOT A LOT INVESTED IN THIS CASE.
SO YOU JUST SIT TIGHT AND STAY QUIET WHILE I PEG MY BOUNTY.

"ROUGH TREATMENT"?!
GASP!

YOUR BOUNTY?
9

SOUNDS LIKE YOU NEED SOME *EDUCATING*, BUSTER--FROM ONE TREKKER TO ANOTHER!

WHAM

KREEEE

YOU *JERK*! I WAS *MOVING*! I *HAD* THEM!

HEY, I WAS HERE *FIRST*. IF YOU HAD JUST--
HOW THE *HELL* WAS I SUPPOSED TO KNOW YOU WEREN'T REALLY *WITH* THEM? KNOCKING ME DOWN WAS A GREAT *INTRODUCTION*.

LOOK-- I SPENT ₩5,000 TO GET THIS LEAD. I WASN'T GONNA SEE IT GO TO WASTE.
WELL, IT JUST *DID*, YOU STUPID SHI--
ALL RIGHT. FORGET IT.

JUST STAY OUT OF MY WAY FROM NOW ON, OKAY, LADY?
OUT OF *YOUR* WAY...?

YOU CROSS *ME* UP AGAIN AND IT'S YOUR ASS!

MY NAME'S VINCENT. WHAT'S YOURS?
11

THE NEXT DAY I UPDATE UNCLE ALEX. HE'S NOT SURPRISED I RAN INTO ANOTHER TREKKER, WITH THE ¢30,000 THEY'VE POSTED ON THIS CASE. STILL, HE LOOKS EVEN MORE CONCERNED THAN HE DID YESTERDAY.
YOU DON'T KNOW HOW DEEP THE POLITICAL ROT GOES IN THIS TOWN, MERCY. I'M JUST FINDING OUT MYSELF.
MY DETECTIVES ARE BEING JAMMED AT EVERY TURN, AND IT'S ONLY GOING TO GET WORSE.
HE WON'T LEAVE FOR A FEW DAYS YET. I'LL STILL FIND HIM.
I HOPE SO, MERCY.
JOHN McCOHM
YOU KNOW, IT'S EASY TO BELIEVE IN YOU WHEN I SEE THAT LOOK IN YOUR EYES-- SO MUCH LIKE YOUR FATHER.
MERCY-- I JUST MEAN...
UNCLE ALEX, I HOPE TO GOD I'M NOTHING LIKE MY FATHER.
I USED THE DAYS LAZMUS! SAID I'D HAVE TO SCRAPE DESPERATELY FOR A LEAD. I GET A LOCALE WHERE THE TRIGGER MAY BE HOLED UP: AN OLD VISTA-RAIL STATION.
I HUG THE SHADOWS AS I MOVE IN.
KBLAM
A WARNING SHOT.

I TOLD YOU, LADY, THIS IS MY BUST.
BACK OFF.

K-BLAM BLAM BLAM
RIGHT.

THAT'LL HOLD HIM LONG ENOUGH.

HAVE TO MOVE FAST. THE TRIGGER MUST'VE HEARD THOSE SHOTS.
DAMN! GONE. OR HE WAS NEVER HERE TO BEGIN WITH.
13

PUTS US BOTH AT A DEAD END, DOESN'T IT?
YOU! YOU ROTTEN--
EASY THERE! NAME'S ROGER VINCENT, BEFORE YOU FIRE OFF ANY OF THOSE COLORFUL TAGS OF YOURS.
LISTEN, I GOT A PROPOSITION FOR YOU. WE BOTH WANT THIS GUY BADLY AND WE'VE BOTH GOT GOOD CONNECTIONS, OTHERWISE WE WOULDN'T BOTH BE HERE. HOW ABOUT WE POOL OUR EFFORTS. TOGETHER WE CAN--
YOU'RE CRAZY IF YOU THINK I'D--
HANG ON, NOW. THE NAME OF THIS GAME'S "NAIL THE HIT MAN," ISN'T IT? IF WE TEAM UP, WE MAY STILL HAVE A CHANCE. WE COULD SPLIT THE REWARD 50-50, AND--
FORGET IT!
I WORK ALONE. YOU JUST STAY CLEAR OF ME, GOT IT?
THE NEXT DAY I'M BACK TO LOOKING FOR LEADS. I SET UP AN AFTERNOON CONNECTION, AND HAVE SOME TIME TO KILL, SO I MEET MOLLY AT THE BAZAAR...
THAT ONE LOOKS GREAT, MERCY.
YOU KIDDING? I LOOK LIKE SOME TUVILLIAN PASTRY IN THIS THING.
INTERSTELLAR BAZAAR

YOU LOOK TERRIFIC, BUT, OKAY--DON'T SETTLE FOR AN OBJEC-TIVE OPINION.
SO, ALEX IS REALLY WORRIED?
YES, AND SO AM I.
Scarves made with 100% Trillius Fabric
PRICES AS MARKED

I'VE GOT TO CATCH THIS GUY, AND TIME'S RUNNING OUT.
THEN MAYBE THIS OTHER TREKKER COULD--

NO WAY! THAT JERK ALREADY BLEW IT FOR ME ONCE. I'LL GET THIS TRIGGER ALONE, IT'LL BE EASIER!
RIGHT. UM... HAVE YOU HEARD FROM PAUL RECENTLY?

PAUL. GUESS WHAT? HE WANTS ME TO GO OFF PLANET WITH HIM.. THE VENUSIAN TOUR.

JUST THE TWO OF US, ALONE WITH THE STARS, A ZILLION MILES FROM EARTH.

SOUNDS WONDERFUL TO ME, MERCY.
UH-HUH. UNTIL THE ROOMS START TO GET TOO SMALL, THE BED TOO CROWDED...

IT'S A LONG WALK BACK FROM THE VENUSIAN SYSTEM.
15

SOME OF THE ROOMS IN NEW GELAPH ARE PRETTY SMALL TO BEGIN WITH, MERCY. YOU'LL NEVER KNOW HOW BIG THEY ARE ELSE-WHERE TILL YOU TRY THEM.
SPARE ME, OKAY, MOLLY?
ANYWAY, MY CONTACT IS IN TEN MINUTES. LET'S GET OUT OF HERE.
THE CONTACT IS A SHIFTY LITTLE WEASEL, BUT HE SAYS AN ESCAPE FROM THE CITY IS PLANNED FOR TONIGHT DOWN IN THE OLD TUNNEL TUBES. I MAKE IT TO THE SITE, BUT NO ONE SHOWS...
...THEN I HEAR SOMETHING BEHIND ME...
...AND THEN TO BOTH SIDES.

A TRAP! THE CREEP SET ME UP FOR A FEW HUNDRED CREDITS. IT HAPPENS SOMETIMES-- BUT NOT TO ME! I'D LIKE TO BREAK HIS SCRAWNY LITTLE NECK, BUT IT LOOKS LIKE HE'S GOING TO COLLECT HIS BLOOD MONEY INSTEAD.
17

HEMMED IN. JUST A MATTER OF SECONDS TILL ONE WORKS AROUND FOR A CLEAN SHOT...

BOOM

CLEAR OUT, YOU RODENTS!
BOOM
BOOM

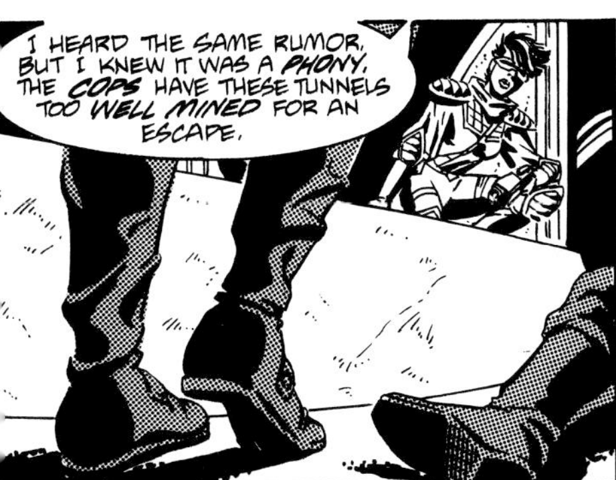
I HEARD THE SAME RUMOR, BUT I KNEW IT WAS A PHONY. THE COPS HAVE THESE TUNNELS TOO WELL MINED FOR AN ESCAPE.

I FIGURED MAYBE YOU DIDN'T KNOW THAT, AND--
YOU STILL IN MY FACE? FIRE OFF OUT OF HERE, PAL. I CAN HANDLE MYSELF. I WAS JUST ABOUT TO...

...TO...

LOOK, I KNOW YOU THINK YOU'RE PRETTY HARD BOILED, LADY. BUT YOU'RE DESPERATE HERE, OTHERWISE YOU WOULDN'T HAVE FALLEN FOR THIS KIND OF TRAP.
I ALSO KNOW TRUST DOESN'T COME EASY TO A TREKKER, BUT I'M DESPERATE, TOO. I'VE GOT NO CHOICE. HOW ABOUT IT?

WHAT THE HELL...

...AT LEAST IT MAY KEEP ME FROM TRIPPING OVER YOU.
19

NATURALLY VINCENT'S OUT OF LEADS, TOO. WE CHECK BACK WITH LAZMUSI. MAYBE MY LUCK'S CHANGING...

SEEMS YOUR TRIGGER'S DUE TO SHIP OUT IN A LOAD OF CARGO ON THE PISCES LINE. HERE'S THE DOCK AND TIME. YOU'LL HAVE TO LEAVE NOW TO CATCH HIM.

PISCES LINE? I'VE NEVER HEARD OF... WAIT A SECOND...

PISCES, SIGN OF THE FISH. IT'D BE LIKE GATEFISH'S EGO TO USE SOMETHING LIKE THAT.

...THINK I HAVE WHAT YOU NEED, St. CLAIR, IF YOU CAN MOVE FAST ENOUGH.

SO UNCLE ALEX WAS RIGHT.

IF IT IS GATEFISH, RICCOVICI'S THE LIKELY HIT MAN.

MAYBE, BUT THERE IS A--

LOOK, YOU DON'T HAVE TIME TO TALK ABOUT THIS. YOU GOTTA MOVE.

RIGHT. WHOEVER IT IS, WE'LL CATCH HIM AT THE DOCK. COME ON.

THANKS FOR THE BLADE, KID.

YOU TAKING ON A PARTNER?

NO, THIS IS STRICTLY A TEMPORARY ARRANGEMENT.

JUST AS WELL. IN THIS GAME, THE FIRST RULE IS COVER YOUR OWN BUTT. KINDA ROUGH ON PARTNERS.

THE EAST-SIDE LOADING DOCKS MAY NOT BE THRIVING, BUT AT LEAST THEY'RE STILL IN BUSINESS-- LEGAL AND OTHERWISE.
VINCENT GETS US IN THROUGH THE ROOF. HE SEEMS TO KNOW WHAT HE'S DOING, I'LL GIVE HIM THAT.
LAZMUSI WAS DEAD ON AGAIN. BUT THIS TIME THERE'S PLENTY OF GUNS ON HAND.
WE SPLIT UP TO POSITION OURSELVES BETTER FOR THE TAKEDOWN, MOVING CAREFULLY IN THE BAD LIGHT...
...THIS PLACE MUST BE LOADED WITH ALARMS.
KLAK
RRRWWNG
THE CATWALKS!
BEEOW
SPANG
KRAK
BLAM
BLAM
BRRRRRT
BRAKKABRAKKKA
VIP
VIP
TING
BEEOW
21

I *WON'T* LET THESE GOONS GET AWAY *AGAIN*.

VINCENT!?

HE'S LEFT HIS POSITION. AND I HAVEN'T TIME TO GO LOOKING FOR HIM.

PFFT

LOOKS LIKE I'M BACK TO WORKING *SOLO*.

BUT THIS TIME I HAVE A CHANCE, BECAUSE IF THIS *IS* RICCOVICI, I BET I KNOW WHERE HE'S *HEADED*.

HIS IS SUPPOSED TO BE A GATEFISH
AFE HOLE"--A PLACE HIS GOONS CAN
IVE INTO IN EMERGENCIES, BUT I'VE
NOWN ABOUT IT FOR WEEKS.

THERE'S A GOOD CHANCE THEY DROPPED RICCOVICI HERE, AND THEY COULDN'T HAVE BEAT ME BY MUCH...
...NOT ENOUGH TIME TO SET A DECENT AMBUSH...

FAKKAFAKKAFAKKA
SPANG
VIP
VIP
VIP
BEEOW

HE'S GOT TWO EDGES; ONE, I'D LIKE HIM ALIVE IF I CAN MANAGE IT...
...AND TWO, HE KNOWS THIS PLACE. THE DARKNESS MAKES IT WORSE, EVEN WITH MY INFRAREDS.

FSSSSSK
AAAH!
23

FSSSSSSS

UUNGH!

HUHH?

OOF!
WHAM
HE'S A GOOD ASSASSIN. HE'S FAST.
I'M A GOOD TREKKER. I'M FASTER.

SSHHHH

LIGHTS OUT, TRIGGER MAN.

DILTON! GET MY UNCLE, I'VE GOT VELANDER'S KILLER HERE! HE'S--
MERCY--
THE PROUD
NOTICE ALL OFFICERS

--I'M AFRAID IT WASN'T HIM.
WHAT DO
OU MEAN? THIS
RICCOVICI, A
ATEFISH TRIGGER.
CAUGHT HIM
AT--
ROGER VINCENT WAS JUST IN. HE HAD THE KILLER.

NO WAY. RICCOVICI WAS AT A SAFE HOLE, AND THE FIGHT HE PUT UP WASN'T AN INNOCENT MAN'S!
I'M SURE HE IS GUILTY--OF SOMETHING OR OTHER.
BUT VINCENT HAD THE ASSASSIN. HE'S ALREADY CONFESSED. WE'RE TAKING HIS FULL STATEMENT NOW.
BUT... HOW DID...?

ALL I KNOW IS WHAT VINCENT TOLD ME. HE SAID YOU WOULDN'T LIKE IT, BUT YOU'D UNDERSTAND...
25

50-50 SPLIT, HUH? THAT *BASTARD*.

I GUESS LAZMUS'S INFORMATION WAS RIGHT ABOUT *PARTNERS*, TOO.

CANTARI APTS
HI, SCUF, I'M BACK, BOY.

BACK TO THESE SAME FOUR WALLS.
SAME SMALL ROOMS.

YOU'LL NEVER KNOW HOW BIG THEY ARE ELSEWHERE UNTIL YOU TRY THEM.

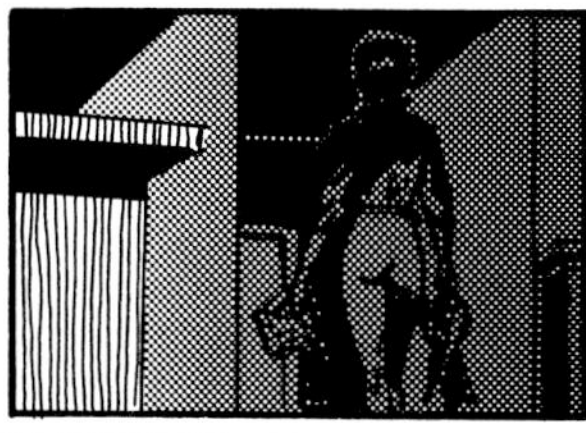

HELLO, PAUL. IT'S ME, RIGHT. WELL, LET ME PUT IT THIS WAY-- COUNT ME IN.
UH-HUH, ME, TOO.
GET OUT OF THERE, SCUF.

BY THE WAY, DOES THAT TOUR GO ANYWHERE NEAR GAMMA 7 ?

GOOD.
NEXT: MERCY in SPACE
IN SIXTY DAYS!

THE JANUS VOYAGE
'87

Story and art
RON RANDALL

Lettering
KEN BRUZENAK

Chapter break art
RON RANDALL WITH CHRIS CHALENOR

SPACEPORT
UH-OH, HEY, MERCY, YOU GOT THE TICKETS?
VERY FUNNY, PAUL, AS IF WE HADN'T JUST COME ALL THE WAY FROM NEW GELAPH WITHOUT YOU KNOWING WHERE THOSE TICKETS WERE EVERY INCH OF THE WAY.

OKAY, SO I'M EXCITED. AFTER ALL, I WAS NEVER REALLY SURE YOU'D AGREE TO COME ALONG.
BUT THIS'LL BE GREAT, MERCY. ONCE I GIVE THIS REPORT TO THE CONVENTION ON *ALVIN*, WE CAN FORGET I'M A COP, FORGET YOU'RE A TREKKER, AND *RELAX* FOR THREE WEEKS, RIGHT?
RIGHT, PAUL. I'M LOOKING FORWARD TO IT.

GOD, THAT SOUNDED *FLAT*-- EVEN TO ME. COME ON, MERCY. WHAT CAN HAPPEN? YOU'LL HAVE SOME LAUGHS, SOME FUN...

LET'S JUST HAVE SOME FUN HERE.
BOARDING SHUTTLE
FOR
DEP 07:25
OOMPH!
HEY-- WHAT'S--
LOOK-- OVER THERE.

LET'S CHECK IT OUT,
HOLD IT! POLICE!
PAUL!
OKAY, FINE, BUT WE'RE NOT LEAVING OUR BAGS HERE!
HEY! I SAID--
PLEASE, SIR-- LET THEM GO. IT WAS NOTHING, REALLY.
YOU SURE, MISTER? ARE YOU--
QUITE ALL RIGHT, YES. I'M AFRAID THE SENTIMENTS OF SOME IN YOUR TOWN ARE STILL RATHER HOSTILE TOWARD THOSE OF US FROM THE MARTIAN STATES.
THOSE FELLOWS WERE JUST SEEING THAT I GOT A "PROPER" SENDOFF.
WELL, THIS ISN'T OUR TOWN, EXACTLY. BUT I CAN STILL APOLOGIZE FOR--
THERE'S NO NEED, I ASSURE YOU. AFTER ALL, NO CITY IS FULL OF ANGELS, IS IT?
I STILL INTEND TO HAVE A MOST PLEASANT VOYAGE. I TRUST YOU WILL AS WELL.
NOW I MUST SEE TO MY LUGGAGE.
GOODBYE.
PLEASANT ENOUGH FELLOW.
COME ON. LET'S GE BACK IN LIN BEFORE T SEATS ARE ALL GONE.

THEY DON'T RUN OUT OF SEATS. A HALF HOUR LATER, WE'RE STRAPPED IN AND LIFTING OFF THE DENVER TARMAC.
IMPRESSIVE CITY, ISN'T IT?
IT'S BIG ENOUGH, YEAH.
THIS SHUTTLE IS SURE PACKED, PAUL.
ALWAYS IS, I HEAR. DENVER MUST DO A HUGE SPACE BUSINESS.
AS WE SPIRAL UP OVER DENVER'S SLEEK TOWERS AND TIDY AVENUES, I TRY TO PICTURE WHAT NEW GELAPH WOULD LOOK LIKE IF IT WAS THE MAJOR SPACEPORT IT WAS ORIGINALLY BUILT TO BE...
...BEFORE THE INDUSTRY WAS MOVED TO THE BIG CITIES.
BY THE TIME DENVER DISAPPEARS IN THE GROUND HAZE, I'VE GIVEN UP TRYING.
THE STRATOSPHERE, MERCY! WELCOME TO SPACE. WE'LL SEE THE JANUS ANY SECOND NOW.
3

THERE SHE IS!
THE JANUS VOYAGE
WELCOME TO THE VENUSIAN CRUISE STARLINER JANUS, MR. AND MRS. AXLE. YOUR PRIVATE ROOM IS... chik... chik... A-27-132. PLEASE USE THE TRANSTUBE TO THE ...chik... LEFT. IF YOU HAVE ANY FURTHER QUESTIONS, PLEASE CONTACT THE--
A ROOMS
B ROOMS
WELL, WE'RE ON OUR WAY NOW, MERCY. YOU NERVOUS?
NO, I'M NOT NERVOUS, PAUL.
IN FACT, I'M LOOKING FORWARD TO CHECKING OUT OUR ROOM.
OUR ROOM?
YES... LET'S CHECK OUT OUR ROOM.
OH.

created, written & drawn by RON RANDALL
lettered by KEN BRUZENAK
TRANSTUBE
LOOK, MERCY--IT'S THE MARTIAN. GUESS HE MADE IT ABOARD, TOO.
HMMM. THERE'S SOMETHING ABOUT THAT GUY...
WHAT DO YOU MEAN?
I DON'T KNOW. IT'S JUST A FEELING, LIKE SOMETHING OUT OF PLACE. I MEAN, A MARTIAN... ALONE ON THE VENUSIAN TOUR?
BUT THAT'S HIS PROBLEM. WE CAN GET THIS TOUR STARTED PROPERLY...
...OFF OUR FEET.
5

THE FIRST TWO DAYS OF THE TRIP, THE JANUS IS ON STAR DRIVE, MAKING FOR OUR FIRST STOP. THERE ARE PARTIES, GORGEOUS SPACESCAPES, BANQUETS, BUT MERCY AND I MOSTLY USE ROOM SERVICE. WE SPEND OUR TIME "CHECKING OUT THE ROOM," AS MERCY PUT IT.
THE ROOM'S PRETTY TERRIFIC.

THEN WE REACH THE ALVIN SATELLITE, WHERE I MAKE MY REPORT. IT GOES SMOOTHLY, AND I'M GLAD TO GET THE BUSINESS PART OF THE TRIP BEHIND ME.

ANOTHER DAY'S JOURNEY TAKES US TO THE LEGENDARY FORESTS ON KRYTERTON.

THIS SAYS THESE VOLLIUS PLANTS ARE NEARLY A THOUSAND YEARS OLD!

LOOK AT THEM, MERCY! THEY'RE LIKE GODS!

I WONDER HOW WELL THE "GODS" LIKE THEIR SOUVENIR VENDORS.

GIVE IT A BREAK, OKAY, MERCY? SOME PEOPLE GENUINELY LIKE THOSE MEMENTOS. IF YOU DON'T, JUST IGNORE THEM.
only ©15!
IT'S CRASS, PAUL. IT CHEAPENS THIS. LOOK AT THEM PUTTING A PRICE ON ALL THIS--"IT'S YOURS FOR FIVE CREDITS."

CHEAPENS IT, MERCY?--FEEL THIS TREE, SMELL THE FRAGRANCE IT PUTS IN THE AIR...

"...NOTHING CAN CHEAPEN ALL THIS, NOT IF YOU DON'T LET IT."

FROM KRYTERTON, THE CRUISE SWEEPS OUT TO THE ISENHOPPER NEBULA, THEN THE RINGS OF NAOVIN,..FINALLY, THE CERSTON EFFECT.
...THIS NATURAL LIGHT DISPLAY IS CAUSED BY THE REFRACTION OF THIS SYSTEM'S SUNLIGHT THROUGH DUST CLOUDS WHICH FLOAT BETWEEN THE MOONS ARIUS AND VILLION.
FOR MOST VISITORS, KNOWING THAT DOESN'T DETRACT FROM THE MAGIC OF THE SPECTACLE!
AMEN TO THAT. RIGHT, MERCY?
VENUSIAN TOURS
VENUSIAN TOURS
MERCY?
HMMM? OH, RIGHT, IT'S...NICE.
COME ON. LET'S GET BACK FOR DINNER. I'M STARVING.
7

IS SOMETHING WRONG, MERCY? YOU WERE QUIET ALL THROUGH DINNER.
NO, PAUL. EVERYTHING'S FINE. I'M HAVING A GREAT TIME.
IT DOESN'T SHOW. YOU HARDLY REACTED TO THE CERSTON EFFECT, FOR INSTANCE. WHAT'S THE MATTER?
WHAT DO YOU MEAN? I THOUGHT IT WAS VERY NICE. I SAID IT WAS NICE.
TRANSI
COME ON, MERCY. "NICE." "BIG." THAT'S ALL YOU'VE SAID ABOUT THESE MIRACLES WE'VE SEEN. I KNOW YOUR THINKING RUNS A LOT DEEPER THAN "NICE."
AND I'D LIKE TO THINK THIS TRIP IS WORTH YOUR TIME.
AND YOUR MONEY, PAUL?
THAT WAS UNFAIR, MERCY.
YOU'RE RIGHT. I'M SORRY. BUT WH DO YOU WANT? I SUPPOSED T WAX POETIC YOU? WHAT IF I DON'T WORK WAY, PAUL?
LOOK, I'M NOT ASKING FOR A PERFORMANCE! BUT IF THESE THINGS MOVE YOU AT ALL, CAN'T WE SHARE THAT A LITTLE? WHAT ARE YOU SO AFRAID OF?
AFRAID? SORRY TO DISAPPOI YOU, PAUL, BUT I'M JUST NOT INTO PURP PROSE. MAYBE YOU SHOULD HAVE COME MOLLY. SHE'S MUCH BETTER AT THAT ST THAN I AM.

MERCY!

IT'S NOT MOLLY I LOVE, YOU HARD-HEADED...

MERCY, ALL I WANT IS TO--
MAYBE YOU'RE RIGHT, PAUL.
HUH?

MAYBE
E COULD
E A LITTLE
RING ABOUT
NOW.

WHY IS IT ALWAYS SWEETEST AFTER A FIGHT?

THE THIRD PLANET WE VISIT IS TRILLIUS, ONE OF THE LUCKY "BOOM" WORLDS WITH A NUMBER OF RICH RESOURCES.
BEFORE WE HIT THE CITY TOUR, PAUL AND I TAKE IN THE FLAVIAN BATHS, WHICH GIVE SO MUCH TO THIS TOUR'S REPUTATION.
The Flavian Baths
CITY SHUTTLE FLAVIAN BATHS
THE WATERS LIVE UP TO THEIR LEGEND. AND THERE'S NO DENYING THAT PAUL LOOKS GREAT IN HIS TRUNKS.
COME ON OVER HERE, LEAN AND MEAN. I'LL TELL YOU A SECRET.
OKAY--AS LONG AS I GET FULL DISCLOSURE.
WITTY MAN.
CRAAAACH

HE'S DEAD, POOR GUY. I WONDER WHO HE--
PAUL, LOOK--
...IT'S A MASK.
IT'S THE MARTIAN! YOU WERE RIGHT, MERCY. THERE WAS MORE ABOUT HIM THAN--
MERCY!
I'M...ALL RIGHT... I THINK.
WHAT WAS THAT?
11

MY BET IS YOU WERE ZAPPED BY A RETTA CHARGE-- AN INSTANTANEOUS IMPLA OF A DATA LOAD INTO YO MIND. DO YOU "SEE" ANYTHING?
WELL...
"...WHEN I CLOSE MY EYES I GET SOME KIND OF IMAGE...
"...BUT IT'S NOT CLEAR. IT DOESN'T MEAN ANYTHING TO ME."
PROBABLY THE MESSAGE IS BLURRED BECAUSE YOU WEREN'T READY TO RECEIVE IT. MAYBE IT'LL CLEAR IN TIME.
ALSO, I GET A FEW WORDS--"GET THIS TO BOLT-- FROM RIGEL."
RIGEL? I THOUGHT THAT WAS JUST A RUMOR.
I DON'T KNOW. I MET A GUY ONCE WHO CLAIMED TO WORK FOR A "RIGEL"...
"HE WAS A SPACE CASE."
THEN YOU'RE A TREKKER, TOO.
HA HA NO, NO, NOT A TREK IN FACT, I W FOR RIG
NOTHING IN SIGHT OUT THERE. IF YOU FEEL OKAY, WHY DON'T YOU STAY WITH THE BODY WHILE I GET THE POLICE.
GREAT--JUST WHAT A TREKKER NEEDS--MORE COPS.
NO OFFENSE, PAUL.
UH-HUH, RIGHT.

AND YOUR LADY FRIEND'S A TREKKER, HUH?
SHE WAS WITH ME AT THE TIME, PAL, SO DON'T GET ANY--
OKAY, OKAY, RELAX. SINCE YOU'RE A COP, WE'LL JUST DROP IT. WE DON'T MUCH LIKE TREKKERS AROUND HERE, THAT'S ALL.
THAT'S NOT MY PROBLEM, IS IT?
JUST MAKE SURE IT STAYS THAT WAY!
WHY DON'T YOU BOTH TAKE IT EASY?
YOU AND THE LADY CAN GO, DETECTIVE.
BY THE WAY, IF THAT GUY WAS A RIGEL AGENT, IT'S NO MYSTERY HE WAS OFFED.
WHAT DO YOU MEAN?
JUST THAT THAT SNEAKY VOLUTIONARY CULT S PLENTY OF ENEMIES OUT HERE.
ANYWAY, YOU US KNOW IF THAT TTA IMAGE CLEARS, GHT, LADY?
COME ON, PAUL.
ANOTHER FINE EXAMPLE OF A POLICE FORCE PROTECTING ITS CITIZENRY, HUH, PAUL?
NOT NOW, MERCY.
BATH 26
13

FINISHED WITH THE COPS, PAUL AND I CONTINUED TO TOUR TRILLIUS. BUT NOW IT'S PAUL WHO'S BEING QUIET, FINALLY, AT THE BEIN VISSAS TOWER...

I DON'T KNOW, MERCY. I GUESS I SHOULD BE USED TO IT BY NOW. JUST ACCEPT IT.

WHAT ARE YOU TALKING ABOUT?

THE IRONY. I MEAN, HERE WE ARE IN THE BEIN VISSAS TOWER-A MONUMENT TO MANKIND'S WORKING TOGETHER AND REACHING THE STARS...

...AND JUST TWO HOURS AGO I WAS HOLDING THAT GUY'S CORPSE IN MY ARMS.

AND THAT'S WHAT WE ARE, ISN'T IT? WE'RE SAVAGES. BRILLIANT SAVAGES.

PAUL, YOU'RE A COP. YOU DEAL WITH THIS STUFF EVERY DAY. HOW CAN YOU BE SO THIN SKINNED?

MAYBE YOU'RE RIGHT, MERCY. BUT LET'S SHUTTLE BACK UP TO THE JANUS FOR DINNER TONIGHT, ALL RIGHT?

THAT NIGHT, PAUL HOLDS ME LIGHTLY AND SILENTLY. WE LIE TOGETHER, QUIET AND STILL, AND THE NIGHT IS OLD BEFORE WE DRIFT TO SLEEP.
BUT WHEN I DO, THE RETTA IMAGE RETURNS.

PAUL?

PAUL, WHAT--?
I JUST GOT A CALL FROM INTERSTAK, MERCY. THEY WANT ALL COPS IN THIS SECTOR FOR SOME DAMN EMERGENCY. OUR FRIENDS ON TRILLIUS MUST HAVE GIVEN THEM MY NAME.

OU'RE
DDING
ME.
NO. I--I HAVE TO GO, MERCY. THEY'RE SENDING A SHUTTLE.

I'M SORRY AS HELL ABOUT THIS, MERCY. BUT IT'S A CLASS-ALPHA CALL, AND--
WELL, THEN! WE HAVE TO GET YOU GOING, DON'T WE?

MERCY! DON'T--
GOOD LUCK, PAUL.
BRING IN THE BAD GUYS.

MERCY...?

OKAY. NO BIG DEAL. THAT'S HOW YOU WANT IT, ISN'T IT?

15

THE NEXT DAY, I LEAVE THE TOUR AT THE SPACEPORT ON ALVATHA. FROM HERE I CAN CATCH A FLIGHT TO GAMMA 7. I ALWAYS KNEW I COULD LEAVE THE TOUR HERE, AND I'D HAD IT IN MIND IN CASE PAUL AND I DIDN'T WORK OUT.
WELL, WE WERE WORKING OUT, AND PAUL'S GONE ANYWAY. BUT THAT'S NOT THE LAST SURPRISE FOR ME...
Ʉ2,700?! THAT'S CRAZY! THAT'S TWICE WHAT I WAS TOLD--
YES. IT'S TWICE WHAT IT WAS JUST LAST WEEK, MA'AM...
CIRRUS LINES
DEPARTURES ARRIVALS
BUT WITH THE TROUBLE ON DELFERON, THE WHOLE SECTOR'S UNSTABLE, SO--
I DON'T CARE ABOUT THE WHOLE SECTOR! I DON'T HAVE Ʉ2,700. WHAT AM I SUPPOSED TO DO NOW?
I'M SORRY, MA'AM. PERHAPS THE TRALMARIANS AND LAVONITES WILL SETTLE THEIR DIFFERENCES, AND--
YEAH, RIGHT. AND I'LL BE ELECTED TO HEAD THE TRIUMVIRATE NEXT YEAR. THANKS A LOT, BUDDY.
GREAT. NOW I HAVE TWO CHOICES: HEAD BACK FOR EARTH ON THE REST OF MY TOUR TICKET, OR RAISE SOME FAST MONEY...
HEY--!
OOOF!
WHAK!
SHE COULD USE SOME HELP, AND SHE LOOKS RICH ENOUGH...

...LET'S JUST HOPE SHE'LL BE PROPERLY GRATEFUL.
SHE AND HER FRIENDS ARE BADLY OUTNUMBERED BY THESE GOONS, BUT AT LEAST THEY CAN'T BRANDISH WEAPONS IN THIS SECURED PORT.
MY OWN GUNS ARE CONCEALED DEEP IN MY SUITCASE.
WHUDDD
UUHH!
THESE GUYS DON'T SEEM TO KNOW KIOVE...
WHACK
...A WEAKNESS IN THEIR TRAINING I'M HAPPY TO EXPLOIT--SINCE I'M NOT LETTING GO OF MY BAGGAGE IN HERE.
17

KRUMP
AAGH!
BRILLIANT!
YES, A REMARKABLE DISPLAY--AND IN HEELS, TOO. MY CONGRATULATIONS AND THANKS.
I AM PHILLICIA LANTICE, DIPLOMATIC COURIER OF THE STATE OF TRALMARES. YOU'VE AIDED AN IMPORTANT STATE MISSION. IF THERE'S ANYTHING I CAN DO TO REPAY--
THERE MAY BE. I NEED ¢1,000 TO GET TO GAMMA 7. CAN YOU HELP ME?
PHILLICIA-- THE PORT SECURITY--
--WILL BE HERE MOMENTARILY, YES. UNFORTUNATELY, WE CANNOT WAIT FOR THEM. LEAVE LAKKA TO DEAL WITH THEM.
AS FOR YOUR REQUEST, MY FRIEND, I'M AFRAID I MYSELF CANNOT CLEAR SUCH AN EXPENDITURE...
...HOWEVER, ON OUR DANGEROUS TRIP, A FIGHTER SUCH AS YOURSELF MAY BE NEEDED AGAIN.
PLACE YOU WISH, PLEASE JOIN US.

I'M NOT CRAZY ABOUT STEPPING INTO SOME-ONE ELSE'S FIGHTS, BUT I'VE GOT NO BETTER OPTION RIGHT NOW.
ALL RIGHT, LADY. LET'S GET STARTED.
WE WASTE NO TIME TAKING OFF. LANTICE EXPLAINS CLEARANCE IS NO PROBLEM FOR A DIPLOMATIC COURIER, AND THE MESSAGE SHE CARRIES IS URGENT.
"MY PLANET, DELFERON, HAS TWO GREAT STATES: MINE, TRALMARES-- AND LAVON. OUR BITTER WAR IS THE CAUSE OF THE ECONOMIC UPHEAVAL THROUGHOUT THIS WHOLE SPACE SECTOR."
I CARRY HERE A TREATY FOR SIGNING FROM OUR NEIGHBORING PLANET, MAL. IT GUARANTEES US THE AID WE NEED TO QUELL THE LAVONITES' AGGRESSION.
SO, NATURALLY, THEY WILL DO ANYTHING TO DELAY OR PREVENT THE SIGNING...
ANTICE KEEPS TALKING, UT THEN MY EYE LIMPSES THE SHIP'S AVI-SCREEN...
...AND SUDDENLY ALARMS ARE SCREAMING IN MY BRAIN. AT FIRST I'M AT A TOTAL LOSS.
THEN IT ALL BECOMES CRYSTAL CLEAR.
WELL, IT'S NOT ALL CLEAR. WHY DOES MY RETTA IMAGE MATCH THE NAV-MAP? WHAT HAS RIGEL TO DO WITH THIS WAR? AND WHO--OR WHAT--IS "BOLT"?
19

PHILLICIA--
THAT CITY ON THE NAVI-SCREEN--IS THAT WHERE WE'RE HEADING?
THE LESS YOU KNOW ABOUT OUR ROUTE, THE BETTER IT'LL BE, MERCY.
WHY? WHAT'S--
BWEEEEP BWEEEEE
INCOMING SHIP, PHILLICIA! WE CAN'T OUTRUN IT!
DAMN! PREPARE TO REPEL BOARDERS
MERCY--IF THERE'S ONE PERSON I'D PICK TO MAKE IT OUT OF THIS, IT'S YOU. TAKE THE SATCHEL.
IF YOU MAKE IT OUT, GET TO THE CAPITAL. USE MY NAME, THEY'LL PAY YOU.
BUT--
BHWHOOM
THEY'VE DOCKED US!

FRAKA FRAKA
BWHAM
BEEOW
SPANG
THIS IS NO GOOD. THE LAVONITES ARE WELL DRILLED AND THEIR HARDWARE'S TOP NOTCH.
IT WON'T TAKE LONG FOR THEM TO ROUT US.
IF I'M GOING TO MAKE IT OUT OF HERE, IT'S TIME TO MOVE. THE LIFE PODS ARE TWO LEVELS DOWN.
I DON'T LIKE LEAVING A FIGHT--EVEN THOUGH THIS ONE REALLY ISN'T MINE.
BUT IT'S WHAT LANTICE WANTED, AND IT'S MY ONLY CHANCE TO MAKE IT TO GAMMA 7.
THERE'S ONE! SHE'S GOT THE SATCHEL!
HALT! GIVE YOURSELF UP!
FRAKKA FRAKKA FRAKKA
"GIVE UP"? GREAT COMEDIANS OUT THERE.
21

KPOW!
BLAM
BLAM

FRAKKAFRAKKAFRAKKA
ZING
BEEOW
VIP
VIP

HEY--!

WHACK
THUD

THE PODS SHOULD BE THIS WAY.

I'LL BE GLAD TO GET THIS OVER WITH AND BE BACK TO MINDING MY OWN BUSINESS. WORKING WITH STRANGERS, THERE'S TOO MANY SURPRISES JUMPING AT YOU!

HERE SHE IS!
HOLD IT, LADY!

OOOF!

UUUHH!
SETTLE DOWN, WOMAN...
GOT THE SATCHEL.
PIN HER DOWN! PIN HER DOWN!

DAMN!
GOOD WORK, LINSKY.
23

OH NO! IT'S *EMPTY*. SHE WAS A *DECOY*!
CAPTAIN! ONE OF THE *PODS* HAS ESCAPED, THREE PEOPLE ON BOARD.

THEN *THAT'S* WHERE THE REAL SATCHEL IS. THIS IS DAMN BAD. YOU ARE, IN DEEP TROUBLE, LADY.
CUFF HER.

CUFFS?
POD HAD A SCRAMBLER ON BOARD, CAPTAIN. WE COULDN'T TRACE IT.
GREAT. ALERT ALL PLANETSIDE UNITS WITHIN THE POD'S RANGE.
OH, NO. DON'T TELL ME.
YOU GUYS *CAN'T* BE...
I'M AFRAID THEY AR MERCY.
...THEY REALLY *ARE* COPS...
PAUL...?
...AND YOU REALLY *ARE* IN TROUBLE.
NEXT: MERCY IN THE SLAMMER! SO WHO'S GONNA TRACK DOW
"THE BABEL CANNON"

TREKKER
THE BABEL CANNON PART 1

Story and art
RON RANDALL

Lettering
KEN BRUZENAK

Chapter break art
RON RANDALL WITH CHRIS CHALENOR

OKAY, OKAY, BOY. HERE IT IS.

REALLY GOING AT IT, AREN'T YOU, SCUF?
SORRY I'M LATE. HAD SOME LAST MIN-UTE CUSTOMERS AT THE SHOP TODAY.

TAKE IT EASY, PAL. WE DON'T WANT YOU TO LOSE YOUR YOUTHFUL FIGURE BEFORE MERCY GETS BACK, DO WE?

MOLLY? THAT YOU IN HERE?
OH, HELLO, ALEX.
I'M JUST WATCHING THE "FOUR-LEGGED APPETITE" PUT ON HIS SHOW.
SO I SEE. HOW'S THE OLD FELLOW DOING WITH MERCY AWAY?
WELL, IT HASN'T THROWN HIS EATING OFF. EVERY DAY I COME BY AND GET THE SAME SHOCKING DISPLAY OF VORACITY.
WHAT BRINGS YOU OVER, ALEX?
COUPLE OF MESSAGES MERCY SHOULD SEE AS SOON AS SHE'S BACK. HER MACHINE'S ON THE FRITZ, AS USUAL, SO I THOUGHT I'D SWING THEM BY.
YOU'RE A GOOD UNCLE, ALEX.
THAT'S WHAT FAMILIES ARE FOR, RIGHT?

ALL DONE, FELLA? THAT WAS FAST.
SPEAKING OF FAMILY, ALEX, I GUESS YOU AND SCUF ARE ABOUT IT FOR MERCY, AREN'T YOU? I MEAN, SHE NEVER EVEN MENTIONS HER PARENTS.
I'M NOT SURPRISED, REALLY...
...HER MOTHER DIED WHEN MERCY WAS VERY YOUNG, AND THAT WAS HARD, OF COURSE, AND HER FATHER, MY BROTHER ALAN, WELL...
...ALAN WAS A GOOD MAN, A GOOD COP, ACTUALLY, BUT... THINGS WENT BADLY FOR HIM.
HE'S DEAD NOW, TOO.
ANYWAY, I EXPECT MERCY WILL TELL YOU ABOUT IT IN TIME. SHE SHOULD TELL SOMEONE, SOME-ONE SHE'S CLOSE TO.
MAYBE PAUL, THEN. AFTER ALL, THEY AR ON THE VENUSIAN TOUR TOGETHER, RIGHT? WHO KNOWS WHERE THAT COULD LE
I DON'T KNOW, MOLLY. MERCY'S NOT QUITE THE SORT I PICTURE BEING "SWEPT OFF HER FEET," EVEN ON A LUXURY SPACE CRUISE. YOU KNOW WHAT I MEAN?
COME, COME, ALEX! WHERE'S YOUR SENSE OF ROMANCE? WHY, EVEN NOW, PAUL AND MERCY COULD BE CAUGHT UP IN A LOVE GREATER THAN WE POOR SOULS COULD EVER IMAGINE!

I'M GOING TO KILL THEM. I'M GOING TO KILL THEM ALL, AND I THINK I'LL START WITH PAUL.
IT'S BAD ENOUGH TO HAVE BEEN DUPED BY LANTICE AND TRICKED INTO FIGHTING OFF UNDERCOVER COPS WHILE SHE GOT AWAY. BUT BY NOW THESE LOCAL GOONS MUST HAVE CHECKED OUT MY STORY, AND I SHOULD BE OUT OF HERE.
I BET THEY'RE DRAGGING THEIR FEET "TO TEACH ME A LESSON," BUT RIGHT NOW, PLAYING THEIR LITTLE GAME IS THE LAST THING I'M IN THE MOOD FOR.
the Babel Cannon
created, written & drawn by RON RANDALL
lettered by KEN BRUZENAK
3

K-CHINK
clop
clop
clop

K-CHANG
IT'S ABOUT DAMN *TIME*.
COME ON, MERCY. LET'S JUST GET YOU OUT OF HERE.
WHAT'S THIS *ATTITUDE*, PAUL?! YOU KNOW I SHOULD HAVE BEEN RELEASED *HOURS* AGO!
MERCY, YOU SHOULD FEEL LUCKY TO BE GETTING OUT AT *ALL*!
WHAT?

WELL, WHAT IF YOU'D KILLED ONE OF US DURING THE RAID, FOR INSTANCE? YOU'D BE *DEEP* IN IT, THEN.
I DIDN'T, THOUGH, DID I? A FEW *NICKS* STOPPED MOST OF YOU. BESIDES, NOBODY WAS FLASHING ANY *BADGES* IN THERE, WERE THEY?
SEC BOX

OKAY, I'LL GRANT YOU THAT. BUT THEY SAID IT WAS NECESSARY.

YEAH, BUT *WHY*? WHAT'S GOING ON HERE? WHAT DOES *LANTICE* HAVE IN THAT *SATCHEL*, PAUL?
THEY'RE NOT SAYING BUT SINCE THE OPERATION'S DOWN TO A PLANET SEARCH I CAN GET OUT OF ANYWAY...

...SO HERE'S THE KEY TO A *ROOM* I TOOK FOR US. YOUR GEAR'S ALL THERE. I'LL BE FINISHED HERE IN AN HOUR.
TOMORROW WE'LL GET OFF THIS MUDBALL AND HEAD BACK HOME.

MAYBE WE WON'T HEAD RIGHT HOME. I HAVEN'T YET TOLD PAUL THAT I'VE MATCHED THE RETTA IMAGE WITH A MAP OF DELFERON. I'M SURE NOW THAT IT'S LANTICE'S HIDEOUT, AND I'VE HALF A MIND TO TRACK THAT WOMAN DOWN AND--
EVENING, FIRECRACKER. I TOLD YOU WE WOULD MEET AGAIN...
WHAT...?
...THOUGH I ADMIT I DIDN'T KNOW IT'D BE THIS SOON.
WAIT A SECOND... FIRECRACKER?
AH--SO YOU DO REMEMBER ME. SHOULD I BE FLATTERED?
NO. STILL SLINKING, I SEE. SO, WHAT BRINGS YOU TO THIS ROCK?
...NO. NEVER MIND. I DON'T NEED TO KNOW.
BUT I THINK YOU'LL WANT TO KNOW.
IT SEEMS YOU HAVE SOME-THING OF MINE. A RETTA MESSAGE FROM RIGEL, TO BE EXACT...
MY NAME'S BOLT. JASON BOLT.
YOU MUST HAVE SOME INTERESTING SOURCES OF INFORMATION, JASON BOLT.
OH, I HAVE LOTS TO TELL YOU-- IF WE CAN GO SOME-WHERE MORE PRIVATE?
5

I BRING BOLT ALONG TO THE ROOM. I STILL THINK THE GUY'S A FLAKE, BUT HE DID FIND OUT ABOUT THE RETTA MESSAGE. AND, SO FAR, I'M STILL IN THE DARK.
OKAY, BOLT. LET'S HEAR IT.
FIRST, I HAVE TO KNOW--DID YOU TELL THE POLICE ABOUT THE RETTA MESSAGE?
WHAT RETTA MESSAGE?
COME ON, MS. St. CLAIR. THIS IS IMPORTANT. DO THEY KNOW?
THEY KNOW I HAVE IT, BUT NOT WHAT IT MEANS.
GOOD. WE CAN'T LET THEM RETRIEVE THE SATCHEL ANY MORE THAN WE CAN LET LANTICE KEEP IT.
AND WHY IS THAT, "MR." BOLT?
YOU EVER HEAR OF A DR. LEWIS RETCHERTON, MS. St. CLAIR?
OF COURSE. AND KNOCK OFF THE "MS." MY NAME'S St. CLAIR.
FINE. WHATEVER. RETCHERTON'S DEAD, St. CLAIR. KILLED BY LANTICE--ACTUALLY TRILMUNE SEVA--AND HER CREW, WHEN SHE STOLE THE SATCHEL.
YOU GOING TO MAKE A POINT WITH THIS?
"A STORY. RETCHERTON'S HISTORIC RESEARCH INTO PSYCHIC ENERGIES AND COMMUNICATION EVENTUALLY CAUGHT THE GOVERNMENT'S EAR.
"THEY MADE RETCHERTON THE HEAD OF A DEVELOPMENT PROJECT WHICH ULTIMATELY--AND ACCIDENTALLY-CREATED THE BABEL CANNON."
"THE WHAT?"

HE BABEL ANNON, RETCH- RTON WAS TRIVING FOR A EVICE TO RANSMIT PSYCHIC IPRESSIONS IRECTLY FROM IND TO MIND, TOOL FOR OMMUNICATION, EALING, AND NDERSTANDING.
UT HE COULDN'T ONTROL THE OLUMES OF YCHIC DATA HE PPED. THEY ST FLOODED UT, BURSTING TO THE MIND F THE STUNNED-- R WORSE-- ECEIVER.
"NATURALLY, THE GOVERNMENT SOON REALIZED THE VAST MILITARY POTENTIAL HERE, IF THEY COULD AMPLIFY THE POWER SOURCE."
BUT USING TWO SENDERS JUST "SHORTED" THE BURST, SO THE OBVIOUS ANSWER WAS A GENETICALLY ENGINEERED BRAIN. FINALLY RETCHERTON GOT IT.
"AND WITH IT CAME, THEORETICALLY, THE ABILITY TO TRANSMIT ACROSS VAST DISTANCES AND NULLIFY ENTIRE CITIES WITH A BURST.
"A VIRTUALLY UNSTOPPABLE DOOMSDAY WEAPON.
"BUT BEFORE IT COULD EVEN BE TESTED, LANTICE, SEVA, AND HER GANG OF THUGS STRUCK, MURDERING THE SCIENTISTS, AS THEY STOLE THE GENETICALLY UNIQUE BRAIN AND PLANS TO THE CANNON..."
...IN OTHER WORDS, THE TOOLS TO AFFECT AND ALTER THE COURSE OF THIS CIVILIZATION!
7

AND RIGEL WANTS THOSE TOOLS AS WELL, RIGHT?
NOT THE CANNON. BUT WE HOPE RETCHERTON'S BREAK-THROUGHS MAY STILL BE USED FOR HIS ORIGINAL, HUMANITARIAN PURPOSE.
SO I'M TO EITHER RETRIEVE THE SATCHEL--OR DESTROY IT.
WHY NOT LET THE COPS GET IT? IT'S THE GOVERNMENT'S, ISN'T IT?
WHY DIDN'T YOU GIVE THEM THE RETTA MESSAGE? SAME REASON.
I BEGIN TO SEE WHY RIGEL'S NOT POPULAR WITH THE COPS.
ONLY PROBLEM, BOLT, IS THAT I DON'T BELIEVE IN THIS FANTASY WEAPON. NOT ANY MORE THAN I TRUST YOU, OR RIGEL, OR THE COPS.
I DIDN'T THINK YOU WOULD. I'M NOT ASKIN YOU TO GI ME THE RET MESSAGE
COME WITH ME IN MY SHIP. ONCE WE CATCH SEVA, YOU C BELIEVE OR NOT. WHAT DO YOU SAY, FIRECRACKER?
YOUR NAVI-COMPUTER HAVE MAPS OF DELFERON?
COMPLETE SET.
I'LL NEED TO LEAVE A NOTE FOR PAUL--
WHAT NOTE? AND WHO'S OUR GUEST, MERCY?
ER--THIS IS BOLT, PAUL.
CARE TO JOIN US ON A LITTLE TRIP?
HUH?

BOLT'S SHIP SLIDES SMOOTHLY UP THROUGH THE STROVIAN ATMOSPHERE, BUT THOUGH IT'S A GOOD SHIP, AND WILL GET US TO DELFERON IN GOOD TIME, PAUL IS LESS THAN PLEASED WITH THE SITUATION...
...SO I'M HUNTING THAT SATCHEL AFTER ALL, ONLY NOW IT'S WITH SOME RIGEL AGENT AND A TREKKER! FUNNY POSITION FOR A COP TO BE IN.
IT'S THE REGIONAL CLOWNS WHO HAVE PROBLEMS WITH RIGEL, PAUL. YOU'RE AN EARTH COP. SO RELAX.
BESIDES, BOLT DOES HAVE MORE INFORMATION THAN WE DO.
IF WE CAN BELIEVE HIM, THAT IS. A "BABEL CANNON"? I'VE NEVER EVEN HEARD A RUMOR...
ME EITHER. BUT A TOP-SECRET WEAPON WOULD EXPLAIN WHY YOU COPS CAME IN UNMARKED, WOULDN'T IT?
YEAH, I GUESS. BUT, STILL...
PAUL, I AGREE BOLT MAY BE "OUT OF ORBIT," BUT THAT'S NOT WHAT'S GETTING YOU, IS IT?
WHAT, DO YOU THINK THIS GUY INTERESTS ME OR SOMETHING?
OKAY, MERCY. SAY THAT'S IT. YOU ARE SOMEONE TO GET JEALOUS OVER.
PAUL...
LET ME SAY IT. I'LL SAY IT IF YOU WON'T...
YOU KNOW WHAT YOU MEAN TO ME--WHAT I WANT TO MEAN TO YOU--
9

PAUL-- THIS IS HARDLY THE TIME OR PLACE FOR--
MAYBE IT'S NOT, BUT YOU ALWAYS FIND SOME WAY TO AVOID IT...
...YOU'VE EVEN USED SEX TO ESCAPE LOVE, HAVEN'T YOU? ISN'T THAT WHAT WAS HAPPENING ON THE CRUISE? I DON'T LIKE FEELING MANIPULATED LIKE THAT, MERCY.
MANIPULATED? I THOUGHT WE WERE JUST HAVING A GOOD TIME!
IS THAT ALL YOU WANT, MERCY-- A GOOD TIME?
THAT'S WHAT I CAME FOR.
NO.
IS THAT ALL YOU WANT?

11

AN HOUR LATER I RETURN TO THE BRIDGE. PAUL STILL CARRIES THE TENSION IN HIS EYES. I KEEP MY EYES BUSY AT BOLT'S NAVI-SCREEN, LOOKING FOR THE CHART TO MATCH MY RETTA IMAGE.

BETWEEN THE TRALMARES-LAVON WAR, AND THE POLICE SEARCH FOR SEVA, IT'LL BE A TRICK FOR US TO MISS CROSSING SOMEBODY'S UNFRIENDLY PATROL GOING IN.

WHERE ARE THE SHIP'S DEFENSES? I'LL KEEP A LOOKOUT.

THIS SHIP HAS NO GUNS, PAUL.

WHAT? AND WE'RE FLYING INTO A WAR PLANET THAT'S CRAZY MISTER!

THAT SEEMS TO BE THE MAJORITY OPINION.
BOLT, COME HERE. I'VE GOT IT.
THE CITY WE'RE LOOKING FOR IS RULVIE.

IT TOOK A WHILE TO FIND THE RIGHT CHART.
I'M NOT SURPRISED. RULVIE IS A MINING TOWN GONE BUST. IT'S BEEN ABANDONED FOR YEARS.
THE RETTA INDICATED THESE MOUNTAINS TO THE NORTH.
MMM, THE TRILLI CRYSTAL MOUNTAINS. QUITE BEAUTIFUL, I HEAR. THEN WHAT?
RULVIE
WHAT DO YOU MEAN?
WHAT'S THE REST OF THE RETTA MESSAGE?
REST OF..? NO, THAT WAS ALL OF IT.
I MEAN THE SECOND-LEVEL MESSAGE.
SECOND-LEVEL MESSAGE...?
NEVER MIND. WE'LL SLIP DOWN TO RULVIE AND GET IT OUT OF YOU TONIGHT.
BOLT THREADS US THROUGH THE DELFERON AIRSPACE WITHOUT INCIDENT. WE DESCEND INTO AN EMPTY LAND AND SEE RULVIE IN THE DISTANCE, LOOKING DARK AND EQUALLY EMPTY.
OH, BOY. DOESN'T THAT SOUND LIKE FUN.
13

SO FAR, SO GOOD.
PAUL, WE'LL NEED A LOOKOUT. YOU MIND DOING THE HONORS WHILE I PICK THE LADY'S BRAIN?
WHAT?

I HAVE TO RELEASE THE REST OF THE MESSAGE THAT SOMEHOW GOT "STUCK" IN MERCY'S BRAIN.
IT WON'T TAKE LONG.

I DON'T THINK DETECTIVE CLEMONS TRUSTS ME VERY MUCH, FIRECRACKER.
DETECTIVE CLEMONS AND I THINK YOU ARE A LOON, MR. BOLT.
WHY ARE YOU TURNING DOWN THE LIGHTS?
SORRY. THE PROCEDURE WORKS BEST WHEN YOU'RE RELAXED. BUT IF THE DIM LIGHT MAKES YOU NERVOUS, I CAN--

OKAY, HAVE SEAT. YOU MAY WANT TO CLOSE YOUR--
WHAT THE HELL DO YOU THINK YOU'RE DOING?
RELAX. I'M JUST GOING TO HIT SOME PRESSURE POINTS.
WELL, NOW WE KNOW WHY THE MESSAGE GOT "STUCK." YOU ALWAYS THIS TENSE?
SHUT UP.
HOW'S THIS DOING?
HEY-- I THINK I AM GETTING SOMETHING.
YES-- A NEW IMAGE IS APPEARING, BOLT!
BOLT--! THERE'S SOMETHING... WHAT IN THE--?!
ONE SECOND, PAUL--
--YOU HAVE IT, MERCY?
"YES--IT'S CLEAR NOW. IT'S A SCHEMATIC OF A PASS IN THE MOUNTAINS. THERE'S A MAIN ENTRANCE--AND A SMALL SIDE ONE. THAT'S THE WAY IN."
15

...BUT THEY'LL PASS TO THE WEST OF US.

THEY'RE *TRALMARIANS*, JUST LOOKING FOR A *LAVON* PATROL THEY CAN TANGLE WITH.

GOOD EYES TO PICK THEM OUT AT THAT DISTANCE, THOUGH.

THANKS.

I'M CURIOUS, BOLT. WHAT WOULD YOU DO IF THEY DID CROSS US? I SEE YOU AREN'T CARRYING GUNS.
I DON'T USE GUNS. I DON'T KILL. I'D RUN.
YOU'D WHAT?
RIGEL DOESN'T BELIEVE IN KILLING.
EXCUSE ME, BUT IN THIS KIND OF WORK THAT'S BEYOND CRAZY.
MAYBE, THAT'S NOT THE WORST WE'VE BEEN CALLED...
...BUT THE THINGS RIGEL WANTS YOU CAN'T GET WITH A GUN.
OH? AND WHAT DOES RIGEL WANT, THEN?
GROWTH, PAUL. OF THE SPIRIT, OF THE RACE. THIS CIVILIZATION HAS GROWN OUT PLENTY-- TO THE STARS. BUT IT HASN'T GROWN UP MUCH. IT'S TIME FOR US TO DO THAT, DON'T YOU THINK?
WHAT I THINK IS YOU DON'T "GROW UP" BY COMMITTING SUICIDE, EITHER.
I GUESS I'LL KEEP MY GUNS FOR NOW.
HA HA! YEAH, I FIGURED YOU WOULD.
KRAKABOOM
17

LOOKS LIKE A WHOPPER OF A HEILMAN'S ELECTRICAL STORM BUILDING UP IN THE MOUNTAINS. HOPE WE DON'T HIT *THAT.*
YOU DON'T HAVE MUCH USE FOR ME, DO YOU, DETECTIVE?
LET'S JUST SAY I'M TRYING TO KEEP AN OPEN MIND.
GOOD. I HOPE IT STAYS THAT WAY!
I WANT TO TELL YOU SOMETHING, PAUL, SOMETHING ABOUT *MERCY.*
SHE'S AN EXTRAORDINARY YOUNG WOMAN, OF COURSE. I'M SURE YOU FEEL THAT, TOO. BUT THERE'S MORE INSIDE HER THAN SHE--AND I THINK YOU--EVEN SUSPECT.
HER LIFE IS GOING TO BE FULL OF BIG ADVENTURES... GREAT HAPPENINGS.
IT'S NOT THE SORT OF LIFE WE'RE ALL BORN TO LIVE, THOUGH, IS IT?
HOLD ON A MINUTE, BOLT. WHERE DO YOU GET OFF TELLING ME--
I THINK I'M ONLY SAYING THINGS YOU HAVE SOME SENSE OF ALREADY...
...THAT YOU, AT LEAST IN PART, FEEL TO BE *TRUE.*

WHY ARE YOU TELLING ME THIS, *BOLT*?

BECAUSE YOU MAY BE RIGHT. TOMORROW I MIGHT BE DEAD.

BOLT--YOU *DO* HAVE GOOD MAPS. I JUST FOUND THE PASS ON THE *COMPUTER*, AND I'VE SET THE COURSE AND BEARING.

GOOD, BECAUSE IT'S TIME TO MOVE. WE'D BETTER MAKE THE MOUNTAINS BY DAYBREAK.

AS WE SKIM CLOSE TO THE MOUNTAINS, WE SEE THEIR CRYSTAL SLOPES REFLECTING EERIE FLASHES OF LIGHT.

THE STORM'S COMING IN, ALL RIGHT. IT'LL SCREW UP NAVIGATION, COMMUNICATION, THE WORKS. WE'LL HAVE TO TRY TO SKIRT AROUND IT AND REACH THE ENTRANCE BEFORE IT HITS.
AND WHAT DO WE DO ONCE WE REACH THE ENTRANCE?

WELL, I'VE GOT A FEW TRICKS TO GET US IN. THEN WE WING IT, I SUPPOSE.
19

THE STORM COMES ON FASTER THAN WE WANT, AND AS THE SHIP'S SYSTEMS FLUCTUATE, WE SET DOWN TO GET RELIABLE BEARINGS...

I THOUGHT SO--WE NEED TO GO *THIS* WAY. LUCKY WE CHECKED, OR--

UH-OH, SEVA'S GOONS,

AND JUST WHEN I WAS BEGINNING TO THINK WE'D *MADE* IT!

NEXT ISSU
SHOWDOWN IN THE CRYSTAL MOUNTAIN
The BABEL CANN
PART TWO-- IN 30 DAYS!

THE BABEL CANNON PART 2
RANDALL
Colwell

Story and art
RON RANDALL

Lettering
KEN BRUZENAK

Chapter break art
RON RANDALL WITH JEREMY COLWELL

THE LEADING EDGE OF A HEILMAN'S ELECTRICAL STORM ON THE WAR PLANET DELFERON ISN'T THE BEST PLACE TO BE CAUGHT FLATFOOTED BY A SQUADRON OF K-127 FIGHTERS. BUT THAT'S WHERE THE TRAIL TO THE INTERSTELLAR GANGSTER TRILMUNE SEVA HAS LED ME.
IT'S JUST ONE MORE THING I OWE HER FOR.
TWO SWOOPING AROUND TO YOUR LEFT, PAUL!
GOT 'EM, MERCY, BUT WITH THEIR NUMBERS, IT'S ONLY A MATTER OF TIME--!
The Babel Cannon
Part 2
created, written & drawn by
RON RANDALL
lettered by
KEN BRUZENAK

PAUL'S RIGHT-- THIS IS NO GOOD. GET BACK TO THE SHIP!

BOLT! ARE YOU CRAZY?
HE IS, BUT WE CAN'T GET STUCK OUT HERE IN THE OPEN. COME ON!

BUT, DAMN IT, ALL THIS DOES IS GIVE THEM A BIGGER TARGET!

OOF!
BIGGER, YES, BUT FASTER, TOO. HANG ON.

CHUCK
WHAROOOOOOM

FZZAAK
FZZZZZT
FZZZZZ

YOU'RE RIGHT, BOLT, THIS BUCKET CAN MOVE.
THAT'S GREAT--IF YOU WANT TO *RUN AWAY*.
I GUESS BOLT FINDS THAT PRETTY HANDY.
WHAT?

AS I'VE ALREADY EXPLAINED TO THE DETECTIVE, MERCY, I WORK FOR *RIGEL*. AND RIGEL DOESN'T KILL.
WHAT?!

YOU JUST SAID THAT, MERCY.
BOLT, THAT IS THE *DUMBEST* THING I'VE EVER--
--WAIT--

YOU'RE HEADING RIGHT FOR THE *CENTER* OF THE *STORM*, BOLT. WHAT ARE YOU *DOING?*
SAVING THIS LITTLE EXCURSION...

...I *HOPE!*
SPRANG
3

GOOD, THE CHARGES IN THE ATMOSPHERE IGNITED THE EXHAUSTED *FUEL*. THAT HEAT CLOUD SHOULD THROW OFF THEIR *TARGETING* TILL WE CAN REACH THE STORM'S CORE.

AND HERE IT COMES. STRAP IN TIGHT AND HANG ON!

BOLT KNIFES THE SHIP INTO THE HEART OF THE STORM AND ALL THE *SHIP'S READINGS* JUMP IMPOSSIBLY.

OUTSIDE, ELECTRIC CLAWS RAKE THE TORTURED SKIES. THE WINDS HOWL AND CRASH AGAINST US LIKE WAVES TOSSING A CORK ON A FURIOUS SEA.

THE RIGORS OF MERE *SPACE FLIGHT* ARE *NOTHING* COMPARED TO THIS HOLOCAUST.

KRAKADOOOM
KRACK BOOM
BOOM
CAN'T RISK IT ANY LONGER...
...BRACE YOURSELVES!

KRAWUUUMPH

ALL THINGS CONSIDERED, NOT A BAD *LANDING*, BOLT.
THANKS, FIRECRACKER, AT LEAST WE'RE IN ONE PIECE.
I BROUGHT US AS FAR AS I *DARED*, FLYING BLIND. WE CAN STILL FIND THE PASS FROM HERE, BUT IT'LL BE ON *FOOT*. COME ON.
5

THEIR INSTRUMENTS WILL BE AS FOULED UP AS OURS, OF COURSE, SO IF THE STORM HOLDS, WE SHOULD MAKE IT TO THE PASS UNDETECTED.
I DON'T THINK WE NEED TO WORRY ABOUT THE STORM HOLDING, DO YOU, MERCY?
THE ONLY THING I'M WORRIED ABOUT IS HOW I GOT STUCK IN THIS MESS.
I MEAN, ALL I WANTED TO DO, ONCE YOU LEFT THE CRUISE, WAS TO GET TO GAMMA 7 AND COLLECT FROM A TREKKER WHO WELCHED ON ME.
INSTEAD, I GET TAKEN BY SEVA'S PHONY STORY-- AND NOW I'M FOLLOWING THIS SPACE CASE, HOPING HE DOESN'T GET US ALL KILLED!
WELL, THIS ISN'T EXACTLY HOW I'D PLANNED FOR OUR CRUISE TRIP TO END UP EITHER, MERCY.
I KNOW, PAUL... MAYBE IT WOULD HAVE BEEN BETTER IF YOU'D LEFT ME BACK IN NEW GELAPH.
NO WAY! IT WAS WORTH IT TO GET YOU OUT OF THERE. THIS MAY NOT BE MUCH OF A PICNIC...
"...BUT BACK ON THOSE STREETS, EVERY SHADOW CAN BE DEADLY!"

I'M COMING BACK TO SWANKY'S, WHERE I LEFT THE BOYS, RIGHT AWAY I SEE THERE'S BEEN TROUBLE.

IT'S DARK INSIDE. WHEN I LEFT, THE LIGHTS WERE ON. SOME-ONE'S MESSED WITH THE BOYS.
AND THAT DON'T SIT WELL...

...THAT DON'T SIT WELL AT ALL.
MITCH, HAGGAR, WHAT THE HELL HAPPENED? LOOKS LIKE YOU KIDS BEEN CHEWED UP AND SPIT OUT BY A CHANK HOUND.

COME ON, MITCH. TALK UP.
SOME HEAVIES... LOOKING FOR YOU, BOSS. SAID... THEY WANNA KNOW WHO NAILED RICCOVICI.

THEY MEAN BUSINESS, LAZMUSI.

RICCOVICI, HUH? I WORKED WITH St. CLAIR ON THAT ONE. I SHOULD HAVE KNOWN HANGING WITH THAT LITTLE TREKKER'D GET ME TROUBLE. SHE'S GOOD AT FINDING TROUBLE.
ONLY, ONE DAY THE TROUBLE GETS EVEN BETTER AT FINDING YOU.
7

KRAKADOOM
BOOM
BOOM
KABOOM
KRAK
KRRRAAK

WHERE'D YOU THINK YOU WERE GOING, PAUL? THE PASS IS UP THIS WAY.
PAUL--?! THANK GOD...

WE MAKE OUR WAY MORE CAUTIOUSLY NOW. STILL, BOLT'S TRACKING IS SOLID, AND SOON WE MAKE IT TO THE PASS I SAW IN THE RETTA IMAGE.

THAT'S THE MAIN ENTRANCE. SIDE DOOR'S AROUND TO THE LEFT.
RIGHT. WE CAN SLIP AROUND THIS OUT-CROP. COME ON.

HOW MUCH LONGER I GOTTA PUT UP WITH THIS?
THREE HOURS, OR TILL THE STORM BREAKS AND THE ELECTRONIC SCANNERS GET BACK ONLINE.

GREAT. WHO DOES SEVA THINK'S DUMB ENOUGH TO BE OUT IN THIS SOUP, ANYWAY?
YOU MEAN, BESIDES YOU AND ME?

HUUGH
9

NEURO-CHARGE. THEY'LL BE HAVING PLEASANT DREAMS FOR THE NEXT HOUR...
BY WHICH TIME WE'LL HAVE TO BE OUT OF HERE ANYWAY.
CLICK
COME ON.
BOLT--THERE'S LOTS OF SIDE TUNNELS. HOW DO YOU KNOW WE GO STRAIGHT?
THE RETTA WOULD HAVE MENTIONED ANYTHING ELSE. BESIDES, IT FIGURES THAT THE LAYOUT WOULD BE PRETTY BASIC.
OKAY-- STRAIGHT ON DOWN. AND LET'S HOPE THE STORM'S TAKEN OUT ANY INTERNAL SURVEIL-LANCE THEY HAVE.
YOU SEE, SEVA'S OUTFIT WAS JUST A MODEST OPERATION. ORIGINALLY, HER ONLY AIM WAS TO GRAB A SLICE OF DELFERON DURING THIS TRALMARES-LAVON WAR...
...BUT HER SIGHTS GOT QUITE A BIT HIGHER...

...WHEN SHE GOT HER HANDS ON THIS.
THERE IT IS, BOYS AND GIRLS. A FULL-SCALE, STAR-SPANNING VERSION OF THE BABEL CANNON.
LOOKS LIKE THEY'VE JUST ABOUT GOT IT ALL SET UP AND READY TO UNLEASH THE MOST POWERFUL, UNSTOPPABLE ENERGIES OUR RACE HAS YET TAPPED.
IN OTHER WORDS, YOU'RE LOOKING AT THE TRIGGER TO APOCALYPSE.

MY GOD. IT IS REAL.
BOLT, GIVE ME YOUR BINOCULARS. I THINK I SEE AN OLD FRIEND.

REPORT TO BAZZIN AT THE FERRON-TUBE WORKS. THEY'RE HAVING MORE TROUBLE WITH THE STORM.
EVERYONE ELSE IS EITHER STUCK OUT IN IT OR BUSY PATCHING LEAKS.
YOU GOT IT, SEVA.

BUT HURRY BACK TO HELP WITH THIS BRAIN HOOKUP. I WANT TO BE FINISHED BY TONIGHT.

RELAX, SEVA. YOU'RE FINISHED RIGHT NOW.
HELLO, "PHILLICIA."

DAMN--
St. CLAIR!
MERCY! LOOK OUT!
THAT'S ENOUGH, SEVA. FREEZE, OR I'LL--
FORGET IT, PAUL. SHE'S MINE.
WHACK
MERCY-- STOP! THERE'S NO NEED! I CAN--
YOU'RE WRONG, BOLT...
13

...FOR *MERCY*, I THINK THERE *IS* A NEED.
SEVA'S TOUGH, SHE'S FAST, AND SHE'S IN TOP CONDITION.

KRAK

WHUUH!

GOOD. I DIDN'T *WANT* THIS TO BE *EASY*.
CHOK!

CLEMONS-- I'VE GOT THE SATCHEL--TOGETHER WE CAN STOP THEM FROM--
SORRY IF IT GOES AGAINST YOUR PACIFIST PRINCIPLES, BOLT-- BUT, LIKE I SAID, I DON'T THINK MERCY'S LOOKING FOR OUR HELP.
CLANG!

YOU'RE DAMN RIGHT I'M NOT. THIS IS BETWEEN SEVA AND ME.
I CALL IT SETTLING A SCORE, AND I'M HAVING A GREAT TIME.
SPLANG

YOU'RE A SIMPLE-MINDED PATSY, ST. CLAIR-- NOW YOU'LL DIE LIKE ONE.

YOU DON'T WANT TO STOP THIS, PAUL? IN GOD'S NAME-- WHY NOT?

HOW CAN IT BE YOU ENJOY WATCHING THIS?
15

CLANG!

YOU CAN STOP THE *PREACHING* NOW, BOLT, IT'S OVER...

...ISN'T IT, SEVA?

HUAAAAGH!

GHAAAAAAAAAAAAAaaaaa...
klikkk
THAT DISPLAY WILL BRING THEM RUNNING.
COME ON, MERCY-- WE GOTTA MOVE!
CLEMONS..? WHAT ARE YOU--?
YOU WANT TO GET OUT OF THIS THING ALIVE, BOLT, WE'LL NEED A DIVERSION.
LET'S GO!
17

KRABOOM

GUESS YOU'RE *RIGHT*, PAUL. THEY'RE SO BUSY PUTTING OUT THAT FIRE WE SHOULD HAVE CLEAR SAILING.

JUST A SECOND, BOLT...

...I NEED YOU TO GIVE ME THAT *SATCHEL* NOW, BEFORE WE GET OUTSIDE.

I CAN'T RISK LOSING IT IN THAT *STORM*.

WHAT?! PAUL, WHAT DO YOU THINK--

OR RISK *ME* LOSING YOU, THAT IT, PAUL? I SEE.

BUT I THINK YOU KNOW I CAN'T LET YOU TAKE IT.

HAVE YOU GONE *MAD*, PAUL THIS ISN'T T TIME OR PL TO--

I WON'T ARGUE THIS, BOLT. I'M LEAVING HERE WITH THE SATCHEL.
NOT IF I CAN PREVENT IT.

YOU CAN'T.

SORRY, BOLT. I TOLD YOU BACK IN RULVIE IT WAS CRAZY TO COME HERE WITHOUT A GUN.
YOU'LL HAVE TO USE IT, PAUL.
DAMN YOU, BOLT...
...DON'T MAKE ME--

MERCY?!
19

MERCY--DO YOU KNOW WHAT YOU'VE THROWN AWAY?
YOU GOING TO BUST ME, PAUL?
OR YOU BOLT? I'VE THROWN AWAY YOUR "MIRACLES," WILL YOU DAMN ME NOW?

"DAMN YOU, MERCY? NO. IN FACT, MAYBE YOU MORE DESERVE OUR THANKS..."

...MAYBE YOU MADE THE ONLY SANE CHOICE POSSIBLE.

WE SLIP OFF PLANET IN BOLT'S SHIP AND DROP PAUL OFF AT THE NEAREST SPACEPORT, SINCE HE'S DUE BACK ON EARTH. HE'S NOT VERY HAPPY WITH MY SOLUTION TO THE CANNON, BUT I CAN'T WORRY ABOUT THAT NOW. BOLT SAYS HE'S HEADING BY GAMMA 7, AND I HAVE ANOTHER SCORE TO SETTLE THERE.

With this issue we reluctantly bring to a close the first series of full-length *Trekker* stories. But the adventures of Mercy St. Clair will continue soon in the pages of *Dark Horse Presents*.

VINCENT'S SHARE

Story and art
RON RANDALL

Lettering
KEN BRUZENAK

Chapter break art
RON RANDALL WITH CHRIS CHALENOR

IN 2226, GAMMA 7 DANGLES AT THE END OF ONE OF THE MANY CHAINS OF SATELLITE COLONIES MAN HAS STRUNG OUT IN HIS TRAVELS THROUGH THE STARS.
GAMMA 7 IS AS FAR AS MAN WENT ON THIS ROUTE BEFORE HE GOT BORED, GAVE UP, AND TURNED BACK.

THAT SENSE OF FAILED PROMISES AND UNFINISHED BUSINESS HANGS HEAVY IN THE AIR HERE, AND EVEN THE BUSIEST AVENUES SEEM TAINTED WITH A LABEL OF "DEAD END."

IT'S AN ATMOSPHERE I'M USED TO. I'M ROGER VINCENT-- A TREKKER. AND I'VE GOT MY OWN SHARE OF LOOSE ENDS THAT NEED TYING UP.

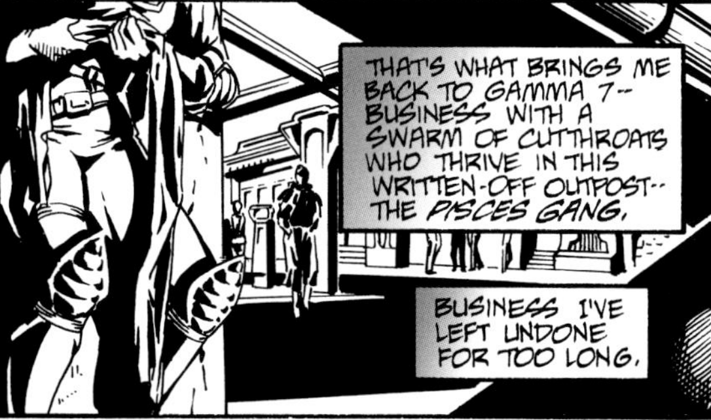
THAT'S WHAT BRINGS ME BACK TO GAMMA 7-- BUSINESS WITH A SWARM OF CUTTHROATS WHO THRIVE IN THIS WRITTEN-OFF OUTPOST-- THE PISCES GANG.
BUSINESS I'VE LEFT UNDONE FOR TOO LONG.

BECAUSE WHEN A TREKKER LEAVES LOOSE ENDS LYING AROUND, SOONER OR LATER THEY COME BACK TO SNARE YOU.

WURRRG

Story & Art by **Ron Randall**
Lettering by **Ken Bruzenak**

WEIGHTED CAPE, YOU'RE GETTING SMOOTHER ALL THE TIME, MERCY.
HOW'D YOU FIND ME?
THE COPS, THEY HAD TO HOLD MY .34 PUMP RIFLE, BUT THEY STILL GAVE ME YOUR ADDRESS ONCE THEY FOUND I HAVE AN UNCLE ON THE FORCE BACK ON EARTH. YOU MAY REMEMBER HIM...
...HE'S THE ONE YOU LIED TO WHEN YOU TOOK THE WHOLE REWARD MONEY THAT WE WERE GOING TO SPLIT FIFTY-FIFTY.
IT ALL COMING BACK TO YOU, ACE?
HEY-- TAKE IT EASY, MERCY...
...I ALWAYS PLANNED TO PAY YOU BACK! YOU DIDN'T NEED TO COME COLLECTING. HOW'D YOU GET WAY OUT HERE, ANYHOW?
WHAT DOES THAT MATTER? I HITCHED A RIDE. NOW--
HITCHED? ST HAVE BEEN INTERESTING OT WHO'D COME BY WAY OF AMMA 7.
HE WAS A SPACE CASE. DON'T CHANGE THE SUBJECT...
ITV ITV
126 STATION 126
ENTER
...I WANT MY MONEY...
3

...OR I WANT HIS SKIN.
THANKS FOR THE RIDE, BOLT.
MERCY, I UNDERSTAND THAT THIS VINCENT FELLOW BURNED YOU. BUT IN MY EXPERIENCE, REVENGE IS A DANGEROUS MOTIVATOR, AND IT USUALLY LEADS TO A BAD ENDING.

HOLD IT. YOU'RE THINKING ABOUT SEVA BACK ON DELFERON, AREN'T YOU?
PARTLY, YES. HER DEATH COULD HAVE BEEN AVOIDED. IT WASN'T NECESSARY TO--

OH, RIGHT, BOLT. THIS FROM THE MAN WHO WAS READY TO THROW HIS OWN LIFE AWAY IN A FUTILE GESTURE OF EMPTY HEROICS.
YOU WEREN'T GOING TO TALK PAUL OUT OF TAKING THAT SATCHEL, YOU KNOW.
YOU'RE THE ONE WH WAS ASKING F A STUPID, PO LESS DEATH

MAYBE THAT'S WHAT YOU SAW--ON AN IMMEDIATE LEVEL, MERCY. BUT TO ME IT WAS ANYTHING BUT POINTLESS!
TO ME, THERE WAS A LEVEL BEYOND PAUL'S PISTOL--A DEEPER SIGNIFICANCE.
4

DON'T YOU SEE, MERCY, THAT SOMETIM WE HAVE TO LIVE BEYOND THE REAC OF OUR FINGERTI

I DIDN'T ANSWER BOLT'S QUESTION. WHY SHOULD I ?
I WATCHED HIS SHIP CUT THROUGH THE PURPLE SMEAR OF GAMMA 7'S MANUFACTURED ATMOSPHERE AND REMINDED MYSELF THAT MY WORLD OPERATES ON PRECISELY WHAT YOU CAN FEEL, WHAT YOU CAN GRAB HOLD OF...
...WHAT YOU CAN TAKE DIRECT AIM AT.
LOOK, MERCY-- I HAVEN'T GOT YOUR MONEY YET-- BUT I'VE GOT SOMETHING BETTER.
I VERY MUCH DOUBT THAT, VINCENT...
...YOU RAN OUT ON ME. I'VE NO REASON TO TRUST YOU.
GIVE ME A CHANCE. I'VE BEEN WORKING ON A BUST-- AND NOW THAT YOU'RE HERE, WE CAN TURN THAT ©15,000 INTO FIVE TIMES AS MUCH! JUST HEAR ME OUT.
THE BAREST CHANCE AT ©75,000 IS HARD TO PASS ON, ESPECIALLY IF YOU'RE A BROKE TREKKER, LIKE ME. SO I DECIDE WE'LL CONTINUE TO TALK. WE MOVE TO VINCENT'S FLOP.
NICE PLACE, VINCENT. SURE LOOKS TO ME LIKE YOU'RE ABOUT READY TO MAKE A FORTUNE.
I MAY SURPRISE YOU, MERCY. I HAD TO LEAVE YOU BACK IN NEW GELAPH TO FOLLOW THAT RAVCOS TRIGGER I'D SPOTTED. IN A MINUTE, YOU'LL BE THANKFUL THAT I DID...
5

"...BECAUSE AS I WAS GETTING READY TO JUMP HIM, JUST WHEN HE'D REACHED HIS SAFE HOLE..."
YOU JERKS HAVE BLOWN IT AGAIN! I GOT TO MEET DAKKON AT 13:25 ON FRIDAY, AND IT'S YOUR JOB TO GET ME THERE!
YOU'D BETTER HAVE ANOTHER ROUTE PLANNED, OR--
"I'D HEARD ENOUGH."
RELAX, TRIGGER. YOU'RE GOING NOWHERE.
WHA--?
"I WASN'T TAKING ANY CHANCES ON LOSING THIS BUST..."
HEY! DON'T LET THAT LITTLE SHIV GET AWAY!
"...BECAUSE, FROM WHAT I'D JUST HEARD, I KNEW I COULD TURN THAT © 30,000 INTO A MUCH BIGGER JACK-POT FOR US."
"JACKPOT"? FOR "US"? THIS CROCK JUST GETS BETTER AND BETTER, VINCENT.
GLAD YOU THINK SO, BECAUSE DAKKON IS A PISCES MAN, I KNEW HE'D BE MY LEAD TO CRACKING THAT GANG...
...IF I COULD EVER FIND HIM. AND NOW I HAD THE MEANS. BUT I HAD TO MOVE FAST.

"IT COST THE WHOLE ©30,000 TO GET BACK TO GAMMA 7 IN TIME. I KNEW JUST WHERE DAKKON WOULD MEET AN INCOMING TRIGGER, AND SURE ENOUGH...
"DAKKON WAS SO MAD THE TRIGGER DIDN'T SHOW THAT IT WAS EASY TO TAIL HIM RIGHT TO THE PISCES SETUP."

IT'S A BEAUTY, BUT I SAW RIGHT AWAY I COULDN'T TAKE THEM DOWN ALONE, SO I'VE BEEN WORKING ON HOW TO SWING IT.
NOW THAT YOU'VE SHOWN UP, WE CAN NAIL THEM-- TOGETHER!
WHAT!?

YOU THINK I'D WORK WITH YOU AGAIN? YOU'RE NUTS, VINCENT!
DAMNED IF YOU AREN'T AS PIGHEADED AS EVER, ST. CLAIR!
YOU WOULDN'T TRUST YOUR OWN SHADOW TO FOLLOW YOU.

THE REWARD FOR THIS PISCES BUST IS JUST WAITING TO BE PLUCKED UP...

...AND THE WAY I SEE IT, WE'RE STILL A TEAM ON THIS CASE. AT LEAST LET ME SHOW YOU THEIR WORKS.
YOU STILL WANT TO PEG ME THEN, YOU'LL BE WELCOME TO TRY. DEAL?

OKAY, VINCENT.
CONVINCE ME.

"AFTER ALL, YOU'RE STILL MY BEST BET FOR GETTING BACK TO NEW GELAPH."

KNOCK
KNOCK

WELL, WELL, RIGHT ON TIME. COM IN, COME IN. ALWAYS NICE TO HAVE VISITOR FROM OUT OF TOWN.

CUT THE CRAP, LAZMUSI. YOU'RE BOILING AT THE NUMBER WE DID ON YOUR STOOGES THE OTHER NIGHT, AND WE KNOW IT.
BUT THAT'S JUST A TASTE OF WHAT'S COMING IF WE DON'T HEAR WHO PINNED RICCOVICI. WHO WAS IT?

RELAX, BOYS. YOU LOOK NERVOUS. WHY DON'T YOU HAVE A SEAT?
BUT I'M AFRAID I CAN'T HELP YOU ON RICCOVICI.
LIKE HELL YOU CAN'T. YO A DAMN NE NETWORK IN THESE STREE
I'M WARNING LAZMUSI

YOU WARNING ME?

I DON'T THINK YOU WANT TO DO THAT, BOYS. NOT WISE. NOT POLITIC.

YOU'VE USED UP YOUR GOODWILL MITCH, SHOW THEM OUT.
YOU F STUP

FOR A MINUTE I'M THINKING MAYBE HE'S DUMBER THAN HE LOOKS. MAYBE THEY'LL PULL THEIR PIECES.
THEN I GUESS HE GETS A FLASH OF THIS ROOM IN BUCKETS OF BLOOD WITH TEN CORPSES FOR FURNITURE HIS BEING ONE OF THEM. ANYWAY, HIS HANDS STOP REACHING.

THIS ISN'T OVER, LAZMUSI. I WOULDN'T WALK THE STREETS ALONE IF I WAS YOU.

THIS IS BAD, ALL RIGHT. THESE BOYS MUST BELONG TO GATEFISH STRAUSS, AND THEY'LL EVEN-TUALLY TRACK THAT BUST TO ST. CLAIR.
THAT'D BE IT FOR THE KID, AND COMPLI-CATED FOR ME, SINCE I HELPED HER ON IT.

THESE SHARKS HAVE TO BE TAILED, AND THE ONLY ONE I KNOW WHO MIGHT PULL THAT OFF...
...IS ME.

TRUST ME, MERCY. THIS ISN'T THE FIRST TIME I'VE "IMPROVISED" IN A DEAL LIKE THIS.
OH? WHAT DOES THAT MEAN--YOU'RE PRACTICED AT SAVING YOUR BUTT WHEN YOU WELSH ON A PARTNER?
KOVO'S

DAMN IT, MERCY, I DIDN'T WELSH ON YOU! I JUST... INVESTED OUR TAKE IN A BIGGER PAYOFF.
POSSIBLE PAYOFF, YOU MEAN. YOU'RE GAMBLING WITH MY ©15,000. MAYBE I NEEDED THAT MONEY RIGHT THEN! EVER THINK OF THAT, GENIUS?
9

OR WILL IT? FIND OUT NEXT ISSUE, WHEN THE ACTION HEATS UP IN **VINCENT'S SHARE, P**

REKKER
by RON RANDALL
VINCENT AND I TAIL THE TWO PISCES GANG MEN OUT OF THE CROWDED BAR AND ONTO THE ITV TUBES THAT CRISSCROSS GAMMA 7. VINCENT KNOWS THE TUBES WELL, AND DEFTLY KEEPS OUR MARKS IN SIGHT WITHOUT THEIR NOTICING US.
IN THIS MAZE OF TUBES, THAT'S MORE THAN I'D GIVEN VINCENT CREDIT FOR. AND I BEGIN TO THINK THAT MAYBE WE'LL GET THAT BOUNTY TO SPLIT AFTER ALL.
Vincent's Share Pt. 2
ettered by
EN BRUZENAK
THEY'RE GONNA HIT THE STREETS. WE'RE IN BUSINESS-- BUT WE'LL HAVE TO STEP LIVELY, MERCY.
THE MARKS HIT A TIMING CENTER --WELL BELOW STREET LEVEL. THE CENTERS CONTROL THE POWER FLOWS ON GAMMA 7. USUALLY THEY'RE IMPASSABLE AND OFF LIMITS, BUT...
UH-OH.
WELL, I TOLD YOU PISCES WAS A BIG OUTFIT. SOMEHOW, DAKKON'S ACCESSING THE TIMING CODES. MUST BE GIVING THEM TIME TO GET THROUGH THE CENTER ON THAT MAINTENANCE SLED.
WE BETTER PRAY IT'S ENOUGH TIME FOR US TO GET THROUGH TOO--ON FOOT!

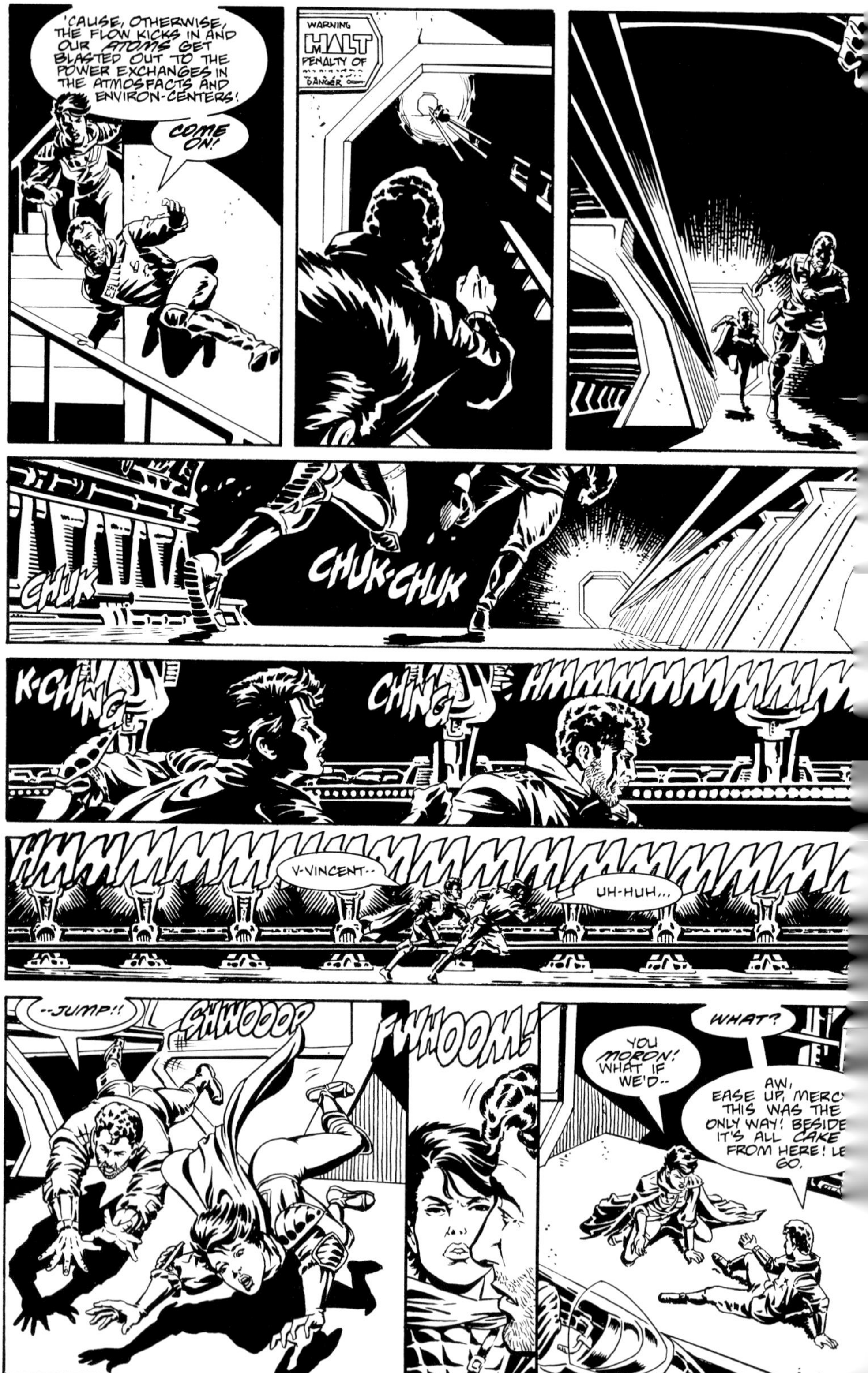

CHUK
CHUK-CHUK

K-CHING
CHING
HMMMMMMMMMM

HMMMMMMMMMMMMMMMMMMMMMMMMMM
V-VINCENT--
UH-HUH...

WITH VINCENT, I KNOW THAT WHATEVER'S COMING WON'T BE A PIECE OF CAKE... BUT WE DO REACH THE PISCES SET UP EASILY ENOUGH...
GOOD, THEY'RE JUST STARTING. I DIDN'T DESCRIBE THIS ACTION TO YOU SINCE I KNEW YOU'D HAVE TO SEE IT YOURSELF.
SEE, THE LATEST PERSONNEL SCANNERS MAKE IT IMPOSSIBLE FOR KNOWN CRIMINALS TO GET THROUGH SECURED SPACEPORTS AND TO SAFE HAVEN--BUT IT HASN'T TAKEN THE MOBS LONG TO GET AROUND THAT... LOOK.
"WHAT IS THAT, AN ANDROID BODY? HOW DOES THAT..."
"TEMPORARY BRAIN TRANSFER. I TOLD YOU YOU WOULDN'T BELIEVE ME.
"IT'S A CRUDE ANDROID-- BUT GOOD ENOUGH TO GET PAST THE SCANNERS...
"MEANWHILE, THE REAL BODY IS SHIPPED IN FROZEN FREIGHT-- UNSCANNED. THEN THEY JUST REVERSE THE PROCESS AND REUNITE THE MIND AND BODY, BEFORE THE ANDROID GIVES OUT.
MY GOD.
"BEAUTIFUL OR WHAT?"
"OKAY, SHOW'S OVER. YOU READY TO MAKE THIS NOW?"
"WHAT DO YOU THINK?"
3

GOOD, I'LL CIRCLE OVER TO THAT COMP BANK, WHERE I CAN COVER THE WHOLE CROWD. ALL YOU HAVE TO DO IS KEEP 'EM FROM DUCKING OUT THIS WAY.
SEE? THE TWO OF US WILL BAG THE WHOLE PACK! LIKE I SAID, A PIECE OF--
DON'T SAY IT, VINCENT. JUST GET MOVING.
I HAVE TO ADMIT, VINCENT'S GOT IT SET WELL, ALTHOUGH IT'S A BIG CROWD FOR JUST THE TWO OF US TO HANDLE...
...ANOTHER CORNER VINCENT'S CUT ON HIS QUEST FOR THE BIG PAYOFF.
HE TAKES UP HIS POSITION, THEN...
HOLD IT, EVERYBODY! RIGHT THERE!
YOU HEARD HIM GET YOUR HANDS U
OUR PLACEMENT WAS RIGHT, AND, LUCKILY, THE PISCES GUNS SEE THAT. SOON WE'RE HERDING THE MARKS INTO A VAC CHAMBER.
YOU KEEP AN EYE ON THEM WHILE I WHISTLE THE COPS.
HEY, TOMMAL, GET YOUR ANDROID BUTT IN THERE. YOU'RE OUR PRIZE CATCH.
I... THINK NOT, TREKKER.

VINCENT!
BLAM
BLAM
BLAM
HOLY--!
WHACK
BOOM
CRUNCH

NO... YOU DON'T...
VINCENT-- GET BACK-- HE'LL KILL YOU!
NOPE--NOT GONNA LOSE THIS--BUST--
HUNGH
CRUNCH
STOP IT-- STOP!
WHAM CRACK RUNCH
STOP, YOU BASTARD!
CRUMPF!

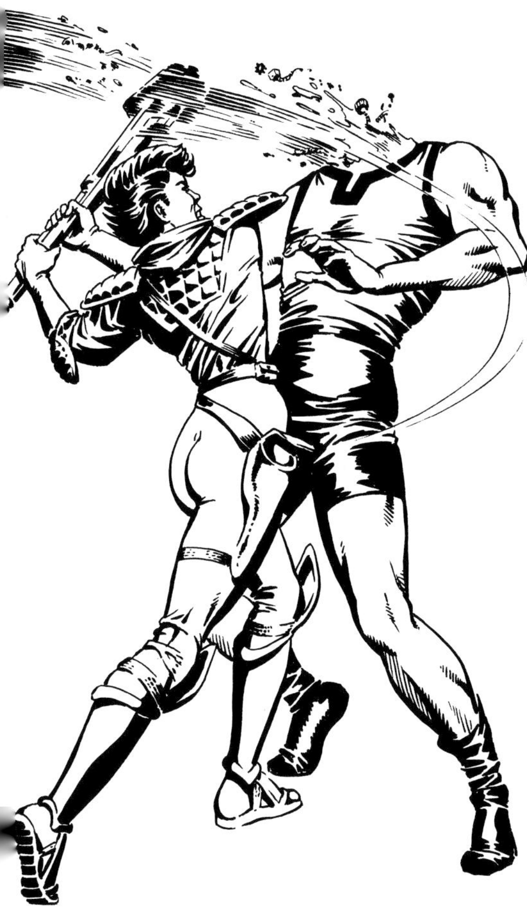

TAKE IT EASY, VINCENT--YOU'LL-- YOU'LL BE OKAY.
:HAUGK:... DON'T... KID A KIDDER... St. CLAIR...

STOP TALKING. DON'T TRY TO MOVE.
GIVE IT... A REST, MERCY.
7

STOP... FUSSING OVER IT... MERCY. IT... ALL WORKS OUT OKAY... DOESN'T IT? ...I MEAN... THIS TIME YOU CAN... HAVE... THE WHOLE REWARD...
SORT OF... BALANCES THE SCALES... DOESN'T... IT...?

"RIGHT, VINCENT. THE SCALES GOT BALANCED, AND THAT'S WHAT I CAME HERE FOR, ISN'T IT?"

VINCENT WAS, AS USUAL, A LITTLE HIGH IN HIS ESTIMATE OF THE REWARD MONEY. STILL, IT EASILY COVERS MY TICKET HOME, AND LEAVES ME WITH A SIZABLE PURSE.
MUCH OF WHICH, OF COURSE, WOULD HAVE BEEN VINCENT'S SHARE--IF HE'D LIVED.

ON THE FLIGHT BACK TO EARTH, I REMEMBER BOLT'S TALK ABOUT THE HAZARDS OF REVENGE. WAS HE RIGHT? AM I, SOMEHOW, RESPONSIBLE FOR VINCENT'S DEATH ...

...OR WAS IT JUST TIME FOR ROGER VINCENT TO PAY UP FOR A LIFETIME OF CUT CORNERS?
THE STARS AREN'T OFFERING ANY ANSWERS. BUT I'M SUDDENLY STRUCK BY THEIR PURITY, AND THE STARKNESS WITH WHICH THEY BURN ON...

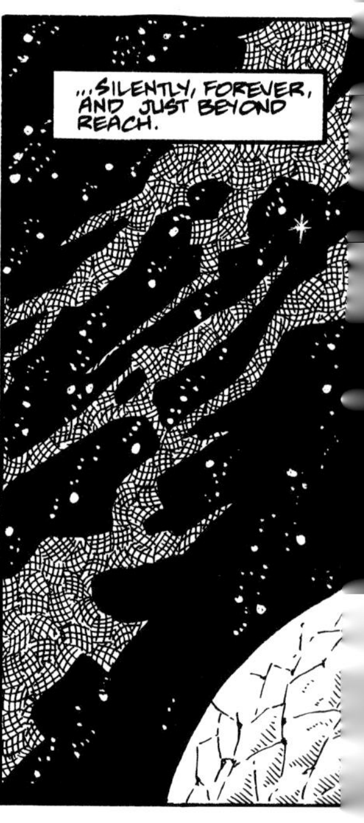
...SILENTLY, FOREVER, AND JUST BEYOND REACH.

INTERLUDE 1: CHINKS

Story and layouts
RON RANDALL

Finishes
DAVE DORMAN AND LURENE HAINES

Lettering
KEN BRUZENAK

Chapter break art
DAVE DORMAN

TREKKER
THE WAITER'S SUIT IS NEAT AS A PIN, EXCEPT FOR THE SMALL STAIN ON ONE ELBOW AND THE PANT CREASES SLIGHTLY OFF. SMALL ENOUGH FLAWS TO GO UNNOTICED BUT FOR CHANCE, OR, PERHAPS, LUCK.
THE MEAL WAS...?
EVERYTHING WAS FINE, THANKS.
THAT'S THE WAY MY MIND'S BEEN RUNNING, EVER SINCE THE STARLINER LIFTED OFF GAMMA 7 AND I LEFT VINCENT'S BODY BEHIND.
I'VE BEEN THINKING ABOUT THE TELLING LITTLE FLAWS. THE CHINKS IN THE ARMOR THAT ARE SO EASY TO LET SLIP BY-- AND THE COSTS YOU PAY FOR THAT NEGLECT.
Chinks
story and breakdowns:
Ron Randall
finished art:
Dave Dorman
art assist:
Lurene Haines
Lettering:
Ken Bruzenak

LIKE THIS WAITER. MAYBE HE'S DOING FINE. OR MAYBE HE'LL LET THOSE LITTLE FAULTS GO, AND THEY'LL BUILD UP UNTIL HE'S CANNED FOR NOT LIVING UP TO THE LINER'S SPOTLESS IMAGE.

THAT'S HOW VINCENT WENT. HE LET SO MANY THINGS SLIDE, SO MANY DEBTS BUILD, THAT THE ONLY WAY TO GET CLEAN WAS BY DYING.
AND I CAME ALONG IN TIME TO HELP THAT PROCESS.

VINCENT WAS A DREAMER. WELL, OKAY. EVERYBODY DREAMS. HIS PROBLEM WAS HE TRUSTED HIS DREAMS.
5

HE TRUSTED ME. HE TRUSTED TOO DAMN MUCH.
A TREKKER CAN'T AFFORD TO HAVE TRUST--IN ANYTHING.

I LEARNED THAT LONG AGO. YOU LET DOWN YOUR GUARD, YOU PAY A PRICE.

FUNNY, THOUGH, HOW THAT ALWAYS MAKES ME THINK OF MOLLY, BACK HOME. SHE TRUSTS, TOO. WAY TOO MUCH.
LIKE THE SISTER WHO LEADS A CHARMED LIFE.

OF COURSE, IT'S A LOT EASIER TO GET AWAY WITH WHEN YOU'RE A SHOP-KEEPER, NOT A TREKKER.
MOLLY'S MUSIC

THANKS, MR. YOLTIVITZ. LET ME KNOW HOW IT WORKS IN REHEARSAL. I'M SURE YOU'LL BE HAPPY WITH ITS HARMONIC CAPACITIES.
I DARESAY, MISS SUNDOWNER. ANK YOU AGAIN FOR CH EXPERT ADVICE. U KNOW, IF I WERE A YOUNGER MAN...

LESS YOU, MR. YOLTIVITZ. THE 250 FOR THAT YAMAHA MAKES HE TAXES AGAIN THIS MONTH. OW IF DAMUSS WILL PAY BACK HAT LOAN I GAVE HIM LAST MONTH, I CAN KEEP MY DOORS PEN THROUGH THE SUMMER T LEAST.

AFTER ALL THE YEARS SPENT LEARNING AND LOVING THIS TRADE, I DON'T PLAN TO LOSE IT, THOUGH THAT CHANCE IS NEVER FAR AWAY, IT SEEMS.

LET'S SEE... JUST ENOUGH FOR THE TUBE FARE TO MERCY'S, SO I CAN FEED SCUF BEFORE--
MOLLY! THANK GOD!
CLOSED

WHAT IS IT, YLVIA?
OH, MOLLY! I'M LATE TO MEET KIRT AGAIN! TIME GOT AWAY FROM ME, AND IF I DON'T CATCH THE TUBE, I KNOW I'LL LOSE HIM, BUT I LOCKED MY MONEY IN THE--
OKAY, SYLVIA, OKAY... I GET IT.

WELL, IT'S ONLY A 23-BLOCK WALK TO MERCY'S. BUT I SUPPOSE IT'S THE SORT OF GESTURE SHE'D SMIRK AT...

...ALL OF HER EXCEPT THE PART THAT ALWAYS MAKES SURE SCUF HAS FOOD BEFORE SHE'LL BUY HER OWN GROCERIES.
C8E LINES
3

IT'LL BE GOOD TO SEE MOLLY AGAIN. SHE IS LIKE A SISTER. ESPECIALLY SINCE THE ONLY REAL FAMILY I HAVE LEFT IS UNCLE ALEX.
THOUGH, AS FAMILY GOES, ALEX IS PRETTY OKAY.
DAD SHOULD HAVE BEEN LIKE ALEX. TOUGH, STEADY, AND SHARP ENOUGH TO DEAL WITH THE STUPIDITIES AND CORRUPTION IN THE COP MACHINERY.
ALEX'S TROUBLE IS THAT HE SEES ALL THE FAULTS, BUT WON'T ADMIT THE DEPARTMENT'S HOPELESS.
HE'S STILL WORKING IN THE SYSTEM, ROTTEN AS IT IS. HE'S STILL GOT HIS FAITH, I GUESS.
THAT'S WHERE WE'RE DIFFERENT.
THE CALL TOOK LONG ENOUGH COMING IN THAT I KNEW SOME STRINGS HAD BEEN PULLED, SO IT WAS NO SURPRISE THAT THE MEN HAD NOTHING TO GIVE ME ON THE SCENE.
IT'S PRETTY MESSY IN THERE, LIEUTENANT. LOTS OF FIREWORKS, BUT NO TRACE OF..
NEVER MIND, SEFFORT. I FIGURED THAT MUCH.

IT'S A CLEAR GANG STATION, AND THE BIG GANGS HAVE TOO MANY HOOKS INTO THE COUNCIL TO EXPECT ANY BREAKS ON THE CASE.
THAT DOESN'T MAKE MY JOB IMPOSSIBLE. JUST CLOSE ENOUGH TO IT THAT I FEEL FOOLISH FOR TRYING.
HEY, LIEUTENANT-- THIS GUY'S BEEN STATLER-- HE WAS A TREKKER.

GREAT. ANOTHER ONE. SOME JERK TRAILING A BIG BOUNTY LEAVES US WITH ANOTHER MURDER AND THE MOB WITH ANOTHER SMALL ARSENAL FROM CLEANING HIS CORPSE.
SHUT UP, WENTZ. THE LIEUTENANT'S NIECE IS--
THAT'S ALL RIGHT, JOHNSON...

...I'M NO FAN OF INSTITUTIONALIZED BOUNTY HUNTING EITHER.
YOU REMEMBER WHEN WE FIRST CLEANED OUT THESE BLOCKS, JOHNSON? WHEN WE RECLAIMED THEM FOR THE CITY?
YES, SIR, LIEUTENANT. THAT WAS BACK IN '15, WASN'T IT?

YEAH. WE DIDN'T NEED ANY TREKKERS THEN. IN FACT, FOR THAT KIND OF WORK, BUILDING SOMETHING LIKE THAT... WELL, A TREKKER'S NOT WORTH A DAMN.
BUT THEN... THE GANGS ARE GETTING BACK IN HERE NOW, AREN'T THEY?
WE'LL FIGHT THEM OUT AGAIN, LIEUTENANT. NOTHING LASTS FOREVER.

RIGHT. NOTHING DOES.

I DON'T USUALLY SOUND OFF IN FRONT OF THE MEN LIKE THAT. IT'S NOT GOOD POLICY. MAYBE IT WAS THE POINTLESSNESS OF THE TREKKER'S DEATH. MAYBE IT WAS KNOWING IT COULD HAVE BEEN MERCY LYING THERE.

/5

AS I SLIDE BETWEEN THE SLICK SHEETS AND WATCH THE STARS MOVE ACROSS THE WINDOWS, I REMEMBER THE OTHER TIME I WAS IN A LINER CABIN. THAT WAS WITH PAUL, AND IT COULD HAVE GONE A LOT BETTER.
MAYBE ALEX HAS THE PATIENCE AND DRIVE TO PLUG AWAY AT A ROCKY ALLIANCE...
... BUT WITH PAUL, I DID MORE TO DEEPEN THE GAPS, AND THOSE CRUISE TICKETS MUST HAVE COST HIM WEEKS OF HIS SALARY.
HE'LL BE WAITING BACK THERE. AND WONDERING, LIKE I AM, WHAT WE HAVE LEFT FOR US.
SCORE:151
IT'S NOT HER, I TELL MYSELF, FOR THE ONE HUNDREDTH TIME.
I CHECK MY MESSAGES ALMOST HOURLY, AND CALL HER PLACE EVERY NIGHT. SHE'S NOT BACK YET, SO I KNOW THAT IT'S NEVER MERCY THAT I SEE OUT OF THE CORNER OF MY EYE. BUT I ALWAYS LOOK ANYWAY.
HEY, PAUL, YOU'RE UP.

WHETHER I'M ON A *PATROL CRUISE*, RIDING THE CITY *TUBES*, OR BLOWING STEAM WITH THE GUYS FROM THE *PRECINCT*...
C'MON, L--SHOOT THROUGH E LOT OF 'EM.

SCORE:151
...I SEEM TO GLIMPSE HER SHOULDER THROUGH A CROWD...OR HEAR A VOICE JUST BEHIND ME...

...AND I ALWAYS SEEM JUST *SHORT* OF REACHING HER.
POINTS
100

THE *STAR CRUISE* TOOK ITS TOLL ON ME. AFTER THOSE WEEKS WITH MERCY, I'M MORE *CAPTIVATED* THAN EVER-- AND MORE *MYSTIFIED*.
SORRY, L. MY ME'S NOT ON NIGHT.

I STILL DON'T KNOW HOW SHE REALLY FEELS, WHAT SHE REALLY WANTS. I DOUBT *SHE* DOES EITHER.
I DO KNOW SHE CAN *HANDLE* ABOUT ANYTHING SHE WANTS...

...BUT WHETHER THAT INCLUDES A NEW GELAPH STREET COP, A HOTSHOT RIGEL AGENT LIKE JASON BOLT, OR *ANYONE* ELSE...
RICO'S
...THOSE THREE WEEKS DIDN'T GIVE ME A *CLUE* ABOUT THAT.
7

THE CABIN'S IDEAL, THE AIR, THE SOFTER-THAN-SOFT SHEETS, AND THE GENTLE, RHYTHMIC HUMS FROM THE WALLS, ALL DESIGNED TO SOOTHE ME TO SLEEP, INSTEAD BADGER MY THOUGHTS.

EVERYTHING HERE-- IN THE CABIN, ON THE WHOLE SHIP--ARGUES OF A SOCIETY RICH, WELL GREASED, AND RISING CONTENTEDLY TO PERFECTION, AND FOR MANY HERE, MAYBE THAT'S ALL THEY SEE.
BUT I'M ONLY HERE BY CHANCE.

I DON'T COME FROM THIS PRISTINE WORLD, BUT FROM THE CORROSION OF NEW GELAPH.
AND I'VE BEEN IN THE DEEP SECTORS NOW, AND HEARD OF RENEGADE FACTIONS LIKE RIGEL.

LIKE THE STAINS ON THE WAITER'S COAT, THOSE ARE CHINKS IN THE ILLUSION WE'RE MEANT TO BUY.
I WANT TO FIND OUT WHAT THOSE CHINKS ADD UP TO.

BUT WHEN I'M BACK IN NEW GELAPH, I'LL STRAP ON THE SAME ARMOR AND GUNS I WORE WHEN VINCENT DIED... A VIOLENT, FOOLISH DEATH.

I'LL WEAR THE SAME TOOLS THAT MAKE ME RULE OUT MOLLY'S KIND OF TRUST, SET ME APART FROM ALEX'S SOCIETY, WALL ME OFF FROM PAUL.
ARE THEY THE RIGHT TOOLS TO USE TO FIND THOSE ANSWERS?
AND WILL I FIND THEM ON GELAPH'S STREETS, OR WILL I BE COMING BACK HERE--TO THE STARS?

SINS OF THE FATHERS

TREKKER™

Story and art
RON RANDALL

Colors
JEREMY COLWELL

Lettering
KEN BRUZENAK

Chapter break art
RON RANDALL WITH CHRIS CHALENOR

CONGRATULATIONS, ANGUS, ANOTHER FINE CROP.

ALL WE DO IS FOLLOW THE PROGRAMS YOU'VE SET UP--AND LOOK AT THE RESULTS--IT'S LIKE MAGIC!
MAGIC? IT'S SWEAT AND BLOOD, THISLER. YOU KNOW THAT.

IT'S
WEAT AND BLOOD,
D MORE SWEAT.
RUN 'EM ANOTHER TWO HOURS.
RIGHT, ANGUS.

HELL, I DON'T NEED TO LECTURE THISLER. HE'S JUST TRYING TO BE NICE, BUT I DON'T NEED A CHEERLEADER. I KNOW WHAT I'VE BUILT HERE.

I KNOW WHAT I PRODUCE: THE BEST FIGHTERS IN THE SYSTEM. BUT WHAT IS IT THEY SAY? "BE CAREFUL WHAT YOU DREAM OF--IT MAY COME TRUE."
WELL, I KNOW ABOUT THAT, TOO.

I WATCH THESE KIDS PUMPING FOR ALL THEY'RE WORTH TO HIT A PERFORMANCE I USED TO *WALK* THROUGH. IT'S ALL THEY THINK ABOUT. AND ONE DAY THEY REACH IT.

GOOD FOR THEM, I THINK. GOOD FOR THEM.

BUT FOR ME-- *HALF* MY STRENGTH AND SKILL HAS BEEN STRIPPED FROM ME. NOW, WHEN I NEED IT MOST, MY OWN BODY CAN'T SERVE ME.

THE LEGION OF FIGHTERS I'VE TRAINED OVER THE YEARS HAS SCATTERED THROUGHOUT THE STARS, CHASING *BOUNTIES* AND *MERCENARY JOBS*.

ANGUS McKEE
-DIRECTOR-

AFTER A LIFETIME SPENT SHAPING MYSELF AND OTHERS FOR CONFLICT, I'VE NOTHING WITH WHICH TO FACE THE SHOWDOWN AHEAD OF ME.

BUT-- NO ONE CHOS THIS LIFE FOR ME. IT'S NO GOOD CRYING ABOUT IT NOW.

NO GOOD WAILING TO THE *FATES*-- BEGGING THEM FOR--

TREKKER
--MERCY?!
BLAST MY STARS! MERCY ST. CLAIR!
HELLO, ANGUS. IT'S BEEN AGES, HASN'T IT?
SINS of the FATHERS
CHAPTER 1

THAT IT HAS, MERCY. THAT IT HAS. WHAT BRINGS YOU TO A MUDBALL WORLD LIKE VITRIUS?
OOF! OH, I WAS JUST PASSING BY, AND...
...AND...
OH, ANGUS--ARE YOU ALL RIGHT? WHEN I HEARD ABOUT YOUR... THAT YOU'D BEEN...
I'M FINE, MERCY. BUT HOW DID YOU HEAR-- OH, I SEE--GRILLS! WHAT HAVE YOU BEEN UP TO HERE?!
NOW, ANGUS--TAKE I EASY. HE DIDN'T DO ANYTHING.
THAT'S RIGHT, ANGUS WE BUMPED INTO EAC OTHER ON RALLI. I JUST MENTIONED YOU'D BEEN WHACKE UP, AND SHE WAS ALREADY BOARDING THE SHUTTLE.

WHAT HAPPENED, ANGUS? GRILLS TOLD ME NEXT TO NOTHING.
BECAUSE I'VE TOLD HIM NEXT TO NOTHING. BUT I'LL TELL YOU THE WHOLE STORY, MERCY.

IT'S LONG, THOUGH, AND IT'LL KEEP TILL MORNING. GRILLS, SET HER UP IN THE BIG FLAT. SHE'LL SLEEP BETTER THERE.
LET'S GO, MERCY. HE WON'T SAY A WORD ABOUT IT UNTIL HE'S GOOD AND READY.

YES, I CAN SEE THAT.
YOU'RE AS STUBBORN AS YOU WERE WHEN WE FIRST MET SEVEN YEARS AGO, ANGUS McKEE.
WELL I WAS HARDLY ALONE IN THAT, WAS I, MERCY?

SEVEN YEARS. HAS IT REALLY BEEN? CAN STILL REMEMBER THE DAY. T WAS BACK IN GELAPH, AT MY RAND-NEW SCHOOL...

...HER *UNCLE ALEX*, MY OLD SQUADRON MATE, BROUGHT HER TO ME.

HERE SHE IS, ANGUS. MAYBE YOU'LL HAVE MORE LUCK TALKING HER OUT OF THIS THAN I'VE HAD.

BUT ALEX HAD ALREADY TOLD ME ENOUGH ABOUT MERCY THAT I KNEW I'D BE WASTING MY WORDS.

MERCY'S DAD HAD BEEN A *STREET COP*, AS WAS ALEX AFTER HE LEFT THE SERVICE. NEW GELAPH WAS JUST BEGINNING ITS LONG AND UGLY *DECLINE*, AS THE SPACE INDUSTRY MOVED TO THE NEWER, MORE MODERN SPACEPORTS.

SO *ALAN ST. CLAIR* FELT HE WAS MAKING A SAFER HOME FOR HIS WIFE AND DAUGHTER, AND THAT MEANT THE WORLD TO HIM.

ALEX SAID MERCY'S MOTHER MET ALL LIFE'S KNOCKS AND TRIUMPHS WITH A TWINKLE IN HER EYE AND A SOFT, BUT FEARLESS, SMILE. MERCY BLOSSOMED IN HER CARE.

AND WHEN *JILLIAN ST. CLAIR* WRAPPED HER CHILD IN HER ARMS, THE UNIVERSE WAS A WARM, SAFE, AND LOVING HOME.

BUT THAT UNIVERSE CHANGED WHEN MERCY WAS ONLY *FIVE*: HER MOTHER CONTRACTED THE DELTHIAN WASTING DISEASE.

THE ONLY WAY TO STAVE OFF THE DISEASE WAS WITH QUATRIL, A DANGEROUS, BANNED DRUG. TO GET IT, ALAN HAD TO SEEK OUT THE LAFIEF SMUGGLING GANG.
IT WAS A DESPERATE STEP, AND IT COST NEARLY ALL HIS PAY. BUT THE DOSES KEPT HIS WIFE ALIVE.
DARLING-- WHAT ARE YOU--?
JUST CATCHING UP ON SOME OF THE WOR
I MISSED IN THE HOSPITAL THERE'S SO MUCH.
JILLIAN, NOW YOU HAVE A LIFETIME TO SERVE ALL YOUR WORTHY CAUSES AGAIN. BUT FIRST, REST-- GET WELL.
MERCY AND I NEED YOU TOO, YOU KNOW.
ALL RIGHT, ALAN.
BUT AS THE GELAPH SPACE TRAFFIC TIGHTENED, QUATRIL BECAME TOUGHER TO SMUGGLE IN. THE PRICE LEAPED, AND FINALLY...
NO! YOU CAN'T CUT ME OFF! MY WIFE--
SORRY, ST. CLAIR-- YOU'RE TOO FAR BACK IN YOUR PAYMENTS.
MAYBE THE WIFE'LL GO INTO REMISSION.
SHE DIDN'T, OF COURSE, AND QUICKLY, BRUTALLY, THE ST. CLAIRS' UNIVERSE COLLAPSED.
AT JILLIAN'S DEATH, ALAN GREW SILENT AND WITHDRAWN, EVEN FROM ALEX AND MERCY.
MORRISON & CO.
FUNERAL HOME
IT WAS ONLY YEARS LATER THAT THEY LEARNED THE SECRET VOW ALAN HAD THEN MADE TO HIMSELF.

WORKING *ALONE*, ALAN BEGAN TO TRACE THE OPERATIONS OF THE LAFIEF NETWORK.

ULTIMATELY, HE FOLLOWED THE CHAIN TO *CLEMONT VERHAUS*, A NEW GELAPH POLITICAL HEAVYWEIGHT.

IT WAS THE WORK OF *YEARS* TO PEG VERHAUS SINGLE-HANDEDLY. ALAN'S MATURING DAUGHTER COULD SEE THE PRICE HE PAID FOR HIS LONG, LONELY TOIL.

TO DRAW HIM FROM HIS DARK WORK, MERCY PLAYED ON ALAN'S LOVE FOR VIGOROUS AND DEMANDING SPORTS.
SHE *TRAINED* HERSELF FIERCELY TO PROVIDE HIM WITH HARD-- AND *CATHARTIC*-- WORKOUTS.
BUT, IN THE END, HE WOULD *ALWAYS* RETURN TO HIS *MYSTERIOUS* TASK.

T LAST, ALAN'S WORK AS DONE. HE KNEW E HAD HIS MAN. AS GOOD COP, HE OOK HIS REPORT O HIS *PRECINCT* APTAIN.
GOOD WORK, ST. CLAIR. EXCELLENT. THIS WILL BE VIGOROUSLY PURSUED. VIGOROUSLY.
WHEN, CAPTAIN THORPE?
OH, SOON, OFFICER, SOON, I'M QUITE SURE.

CERTAINLY. VERY SOON INDEED.

POLICE
17th PRECINCT

ALL THOSE YEARS... MY GOD...
...HAS IT ALL BEEN A WASTE?
DAD, WHAT IS IT? I CAN'T STAND THIS ANY LONGER!
YOU NEVER TALK TO ME--NEVER EVEN KNOW I'M HERE! I'M NOT A CHILD, DADDY. PLEASE TALK TO ME.
YES... YOU'RE RIGHT, MERCY...
IT IS PAST TIME I TALKED TO YOU.

ONCE HE STARTED, ALAN COULDN'T STOP. MERCY FINALLY HEARD IT ALL: THE QUATRIL, THE SMUGGLERS, VERHAUS, AND THE REPORT ALAN HAD PAID FOR WITH HIS YEARS OF LABOR.
AND THORPE JUST BURIED IT IN HIS DAMN FILE, LIKE IT WAS WORTHLESS.
TO NAIL VERHAUS, I'VE ROBBED YOU OF A REAL FATHER FOR YEARS, MERCY. WAS THAT ALL FOR NOTHING?
AM I WRONG TO TRUST THORPE?

WILL THE FORCE EVER MOVE ON A GUY WITH VERHAUS'S CLOUT AND CONNECTIONS?
AND IF NOT, DO I GO AFTER VERHAUS ALONE, THROW AWAY MY BADGE, AND MAKE A LIE OUT OF MY YEARS AS A COP?

I DON'T KNOW WHAT TO DO, MERCY. I JUST DON'T KNOW.
DADDY...

IT'S-- IT'S TIME YOU SCOOTED UP TO BED, ANGEL. I NEED TIME...
...I NEED TIME...

THAT NIGHT MERCY WAS HAUNTED BY THE IMAGE OF HER FATHER, TORN AND UNCERTAIN--WEAK. SLEEP WAS LONG IN COMING.
AND HARDLY HAD IT ARRIVED, WHEN...
I SAID, "OUT!"
YOU DON'T GET IT, ST. CLAIR...
...I'M HERE TO STOP THOSE CARELESS CLAIMS YOU'VE BEEN MAKING ABOUT MR. VERHAUS.
IT'S TOO LATE, I'VE TOLD YOU. MY REPORT'S ALREADY ON FILE, SO--
THAT REPORT'S GONE MISSING, I'M AFRAID.
YOU'RE A SIMPLE SAP, AREN'T YOU, ST. CLAIR? YOU WON'T BE MUCH MISSED.
DADDY-- NO!!
PAK PAK
THE BRAT'S UP, HUH? WELL, I'LL--
POOF
SPAT
GAAH!

DADDY.. DADDY.. HANG ON..

IT'S... IT'S ALL RIGHT. WE'LL GET YOU TO THE... TO THE...

OH, GOD. OH, GOD.

NO. DON'T GO, DADDY... DON'T GO.
DADDY.
COME BACK.

MERCY.. IF YOU'RE READY, CAPTAIN THORPE WANTS A WORD.
THAT BASTARD! I WON'T TALK TO HIM, ALEX.
HE KNEW WHAT WOULD HAPPEN. HE DIDN'T CARE.
POLICE
DON'T BLAME THORPE, MERCY. HE'S JUST A LITTLE COG IN THIS.
BUT I'LL GET VERHAUS, ONE DAY. I PROMISE YOU THAT.
WHAT GOOD WILL THAT DO MY DAD? HE WAS A FOOL TO COUNT ON THE FORCE! HE WAS CARELESS AND TRUSTING.
NOW HE'S GONE. BUT AT LEAST I CAN LEARN FROM HIS MISTAKES...
...THORPE AND HIS WHOLE WORTHLESS SYSTEM CAN ALL GO TO HELL.

ALEX TOOK MERCY IN. WITHIN A FEW MONTHS, HE ALSO NAILED VERHAUS. THE DEPARTMENT MADE HIM A LIEUTENANT-- BUT IT DIDN'T COUNT FOR MUCH WITH MERCY.
THEN, A YEAR AFTER ALAN'S DEATH...
...CITY COUNCIL HAS TODAY ENDORSED THE NEWLY PROPOSED TREKKER ORDINANCE. THE COUNCIL INSISTS THIS IS NOT A SIGN OF A CITY IN CRISIS, BUT A SOBER RESPONSE TO--
WHAT?!
"TREKKERS"! LICENSED BOUNTY HUNTING IS WHAT IT IS. AND IT SURE AS HELL IS A SIGN OF CRISIS!
WELL, ALEX, CAN YOU SAY THE COPS ARE IN CONTROL OF THIS CITY?
THIS IS NO SOLUTION, MERCY!
THIS'LL JUST UNDERMINE THE EFFORTS OF THE POLICE EVEN MORE!
IT'S TELLING PEOPLE TO TAKE THE LAW INTO THEIR OWN HANDS!
MAYBE THAT'S WHERE IT SHOULD BE, UNCLE ALEX.

BY THE TIME SHE WAS SEVENTEEN, MERCY WAS SET ON BEING A TREKKER HERSELF. ALEX DECIDED IF SHE COULDN'T BE *DISSUADED*, SHE SHOULD AT LEAST BE PROPERLY *TRAINED*, SO HE BROUGHT HER TO ME.

AND HERE SHE IS, SEVEN YEARS A
A TREKKER LATER. THE LIFE'S SHAPED HER SOME, ALL RIGHT. YOU CAN SEE IT IN HER EYES-- BUT THEY STILL HAVE THE SAME *FIRE* IN THEM.

I WONDER WHAT SHE SEES... WHEN SHE LOOKS AT *THIS* BATTERED OLD SHELL?

OLDER.
ANGUS. OLD, ALONE, AND CRIPPLED. I STILL CAN'T BELIEVE IT.

LISTEN TO ME! HOW INDESTRUCTIBLE I MUST HAVE THOUGHT HE WAS. WHAT A PEDESTAL I HAD HIM ON.
BUT I WAS YOUNG, AND HE WAS SO TOUGH, SO STRONG AND SURE.

WHO DID IT TO YOU, ANGUS? BEFORE I RETURN TO EARTH, I HAVE TO KNOW.
WHO TRIED TO KILL THE MAN MY FATHER SHOULD HAVE BEEN?

WOW.

UH-HUH.

Chapter 2

PROG/LEV SCORE TIME
BOXB 1550 37:15

THEY'VE MADE SOME *IMPROVEMENTS* ON THE RIESES BOTS SINCE I TRAINED ON THEM. GOOD. THIS IS THE FIRST DECENT SWEAT I'VE WORKED UP IN DAYS.

YOU KNOW WHAT YOU'RE DOING TO ALL THOSE YOUNG *HORMONES*, ST. CLAIR?
WHAT? OH! SORRY, ANGUS.

HELL, NO, YOU'RE NOT. COULDN'T HELP IT IF YOU WERE. YOU DRAW 'EM LIKE FLIES, MERCY, ALWAYS HAVE.
REMEMBER *KARCH*?

I REMEMBER KARCH.

HEY, YOU GUYS. SEE THAT *GIRL*? SHE'S SUPPOSED TO BE QUITE AN ATHLETE. WONDER IF SHE'LL CUT IT HERE?
I'M ONLY WORRYING ABOUT *MYSELF*, FRIEND. I'M HERE TO BE *THE BEST*. HOW THE REST OF YOU DO ISN'T MY PROBLEM.
HOO! GET *THIS* GUY.
ALL RIGHT, PUPS! WELCOME TO THE *SWEAT-SHOP*. MY NAME'S McKEE. NOW LINE 'EM UP! LET'S GET *MOVIN'* HERE.

THAT WAS KARCH. FROM THE *FIRST DAY*, HE WAS SERVING NOTICE TO US ALL.
ALL RIGHT, KID-- HOLD IT THERE. YOU'VE WON THE FALL--NO NEED TO *KILL* THE LAD.
EASE OFF, I SAID.

SORRY, ANGUS, THAT'S JUST NOT MY STYLE.
NO PRISONERS, NO QUARTER: THAT'S HOW TO HIT THE *TOP*, ISN'T IT?

STOP PUSHING, HEWETT. WHAT'S YOUR RUSH? YOU'LL BE ON THE *BOTTOM* ANYWAY.
DAY 1 POSTINGS--

HEY, *KARCH*. LOOKS LIKE YOU'RE NOT *ALONE* AT THE TOP, HOTSHOT.

"ST. CLAIR," HUH? SO WHO'S THIS ST. CLAIR GUY?

KARCH 1000

ST. CLAIR 1000

BENTON 895

GIOLETTE 885

THANKS.

ST. CLAIR 1000

THE WHOLE FIRST WEEK, KARCH AND I LED THE CLASS, BUT I KEPT TO MYSELF PRETTY MUCH, SO WE NEVER SPOKE, UNTIL...
DAMN BANDIT! GIVE ME MY DRINK!
BAM BAM
HEY.. MIND IF I HAVE A GO AT IT?
I'VE CRACKED THIS SAFE BEFORE. HERE'S THE "COMBINATION".
WHAK
MY PLEASURE. I'VE BEEN WANTING TO TALK TO YOU ANYWAY.
THANKS.
OH?
LISTEN. I DO A LOT OF AFTER-HOURS TRAINING. I BET YOU DO, TOO. I SUGGEST WE TEAM UP. I GUARANTEE WE'LL BOTH GET BETTER WORKOUTS THAT WAY.
WELL I DON'T
COME ON, MERCY! WE'RE OBVIOUSLY THE CLASS AT THIS SCHOOL. NO ONE ELSE HERE CAN CHALLENGE ME ENOUGH TO MAKE ME REALLY HAVE TO WORK.
MMM. MODEST, AREN'T WE?
JUST HONEST ABOUT OUR ABILITIES. MAYBE THAT BOTHERS YOU, BUT NOT ME.
OKAY, KARCH. YOU'RE ON.
OF COURSE, KARCH WAS RIGHT. WORKING TOGETHER, OUR SKILLS BUILT QUICKLY. AS THE WEEKS PASSED, WE BEGAN TO INCREASE OUR DISTANCE FROM THE REST OF THE CLASS.

KARCH WAS FULL OF IDEAS. SOME WERE CRAZY. SOME WERE GREAT. THEY ALL CAME OUT IN THE SAME BURST OF BOYISH ENTHUSIASM. AND THEY WERE ALL ABOUT THE SAME THING...
LISTEN, MERCY! I KNOW HOW WE CAN GET EVEN BETTER RESULTS!
YOU KNOW THE T-BAR ON THE KERTAIN RIG?! WELL, IF WE UNHOOK IT AND SWIVEL IT OUT, WE--
I KNOW. I KNOW. I GET OBSESSIVE, RIGHT?
COME ON. I'LL SPRING FOR A PAIR OF ZOTZ BARS.
BUT EVEN WHEN HE WOULD TRY TO RELAX FROM IT, KARCH'S DEVOURING HUNGER FOR PERFECTION CAME ROARING BACK.
OH, KARCH--! WHAT KIND OF LANDING WAS THAT?!
I'VE GOT NOTHING TODAY! NOTHING! DAMN IT!
GOOD RIDDANCE, NUTCASE!
YEAH. WHO IS HE TRYING TO IMPRESS?

KARCH OFTEN HAD SUCH OUTBURSTS. THEY'D NEVER SEEMED TO AFFECT HIM MUCH. BUT THAT NIGHT, WHEN I GOT BACK TO MY ROOM AFTER CLASSES...
WHO THE HELL--?!
KARCH? IS THAT YOU?
YEAH, MERCY. I'M SORRY--I JUST DIDN'T WANT TO BE IN MY OWN ROOM WHEN THEY GOT BACK, I GUESS.

YOUR ROOMMATES?
I'M AFRAID THEY DON'T LIKE ME MUCH, MERCY.
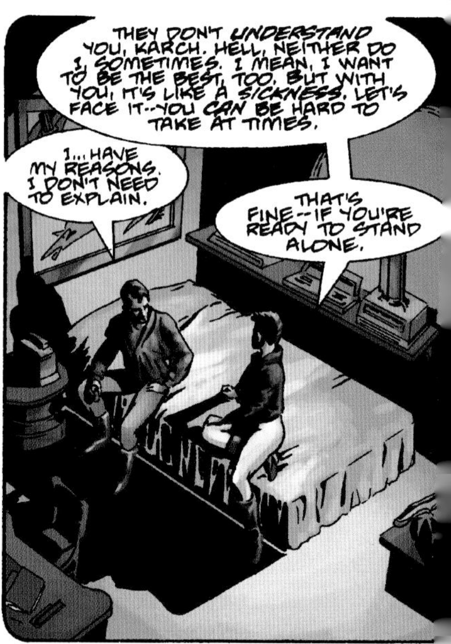
THEY DON'T UNDERSTAND YOU, KARCH. HELL, NEITHER DO I, SOMETIMES. I MEAN, I WANT TO BE THE BEST, TOO, BUT WITH YOU, IT'S LIKE A SICKNESS. LET'S FACE IT--YOU CAN BE HARD TO TAKE AT TIMES.
I... HAVE MY REASONS. I DON'T NEED TO EXPLAIN.
THAT'S FINE--IF YOU'RE READY TO STAND ALONE.

MERCY, I--I DON'T WANT TO BE ALONE...
...TONIGHT.

CLICK

I HADN'T KNOWN HOW ALONE I'D BEEN UNTIL THAT NIGHT--WHEN THE LONELINESS ENDED FOR BOTH OF US.
OH, MERCY-- IT'S SO BEAUTIFUL THIS MORNING!
Mmmmhm...

YOU'RE SO BEAUTIFUL THIS MORNING.
EASY, SAILOR--KIOVE DRILLS AT 6:15 THIS MORNING, REMEMBER?

KIOVE? THIS MORNING? I DON'T THINK SO.
IN FACT, I HAVE SOMETHING COMPLETELY DIFFERENT IN MIND. COME ON--UP!

HE WAS SWEET AND GENTLE--SUCH A LITTLE BOY--WITH ME, AND I COULD BE THE LITTLE GIRL I HADN'T BEEN SINCE MY MOTHER DIED.

IN THE MONTHS THAT FOLLOWED, WE SPENT MORE AND MORE TIME AWAY FROM THE SCHOOL--JUST BEING TWO KIDS.
I FELT YOUNG. I FELT LOVED.

I'D FORGOTTEN WHAT THOSE THINGS WERE.

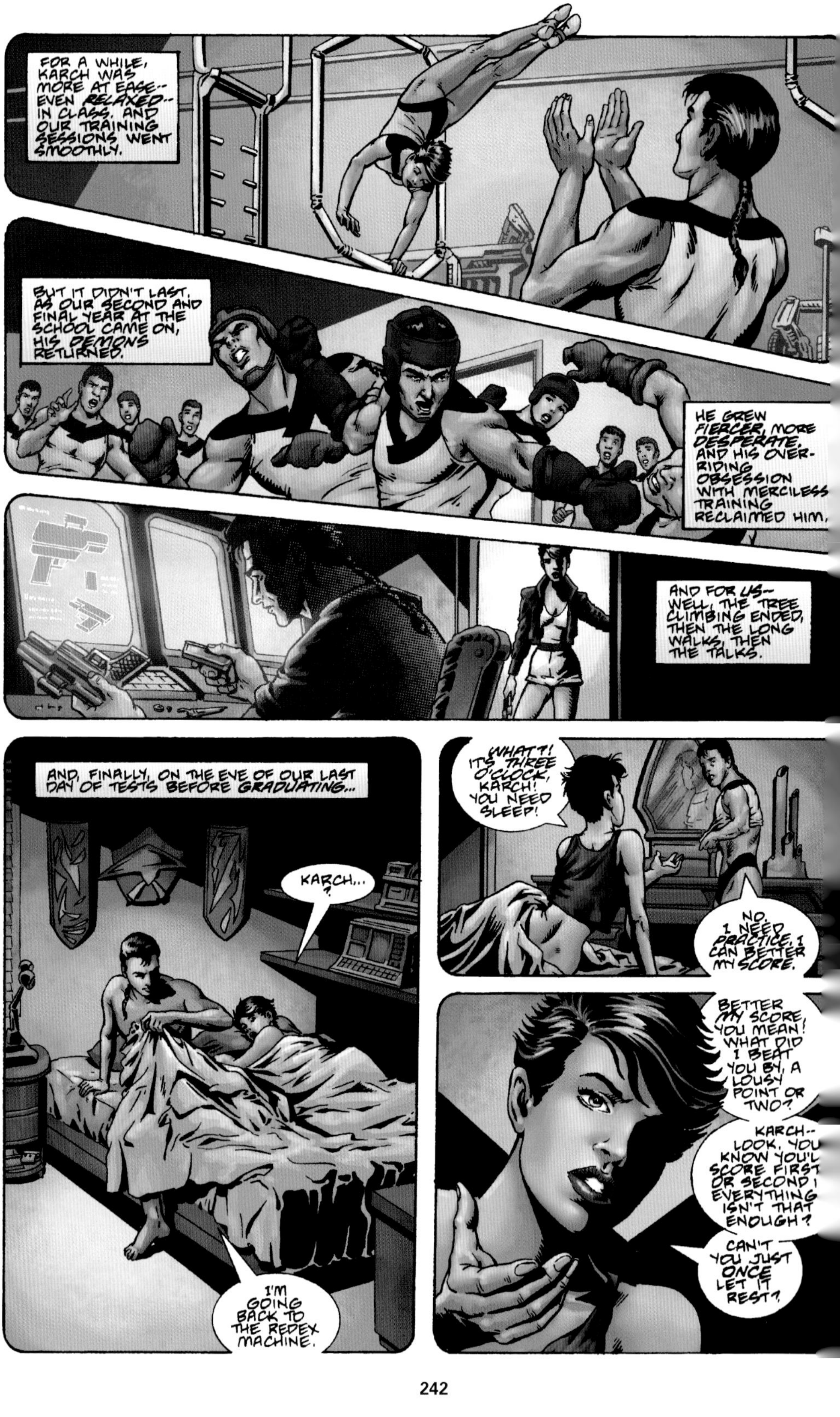

FOR A WHILE, KARCH WAS MORE AT EASE-- EVEN *RELAXED*-- IN CLASS, AND OUR TRAINING SESSIONS WENT SMOOTHLY.

BUT IT DIDN'T LAST. AS OUR SECOND AND FINAL YEAR AT THE SCHOOL CAME ON, HIS *DEMONS* RETURNED.

HE GREW *FIERCER*, MORE *DESPERATE*, AND HIS OVER-RIDING OBSESSION WITH MERCILESS TRAINING RECLAIMED HIM.

AND FOR *US*-- WELL, THE TREE CLIMBING ENDED, THEN THE LONG WALKS, THEN THE TALKS.

AND, FINALLY, ON THE EVE OF OUR LAST DAY OF TESTS BEFORE GRADUATING...
KARCH... ?
I'M GOING BACK TO THE REDEX MACHINE.

WHAT?! IT'S THREE O'CLOCK, KARCH! YOU NEED SLEEP!
NO, I NEED PRACTICE. I CAN BETTER MY SCORE.
BETTER MY SCORE, YOU MEAN! WHAT DID I BEAT YOU BY, A LOUSY POINT OR TWO?
KARCH-- LOOK, YOU KNOW YOU'L SCORE FIRST OR SECOND I EVERYTHING. ISN'T THAT ENOUGH?
CAN'T YOU JUST ONCE LET IT REST?

THAT'S JUST IT, MERCY-- I HAVE RESTED IT.
TOO MUCH. WITH YOU.

IT'S MY OWN FAULT. I KNEW FROM THE START IT WAS A MISTAKE --THAT I'D BE A FOOL TO FALL IN LOVE.
BUT I DID, OF COURSE.

WITH YOU, MERCH. HOW COULD I NOT?

I'LL... I'LL NEVER FORGET..
WHAT ARE YOU SAYING?

I'VE TOLD YOU, MERCY-- THERE'S A REASON I HAVE TO BE THE BEST.
IT'S THE SAME REASON THAT I WAS WRONG TO FALL IN LOVE WITH YOU.
I--I STILL CAN'T EXPLAIN IT...
...AND I NEVER FACED WHAT I KNEW IT WOULD COST ME...
...UNTIL THE LAST MOMENT...
...UNTIL NOW.

I DON'T REMEMBER FEELING ANYTHING THE NEXT DAY--JUST A NUMBNESS. KARCH DIDN'T LOOK AT ME ONCE THROUGH THE TESTS. HE DID BADLY. I DID A LITTLE WORSE SO HE GOT HIS WISH AND FINISHED ON TOP.
KARCH LEFT IMMEDIATELY, STILL WITHOUT A WORD.
YES, ANGUS, I REMEMBER KARCH.
WHY'D YOU MENTION HIM?
WELL, YOU DID WANT TO KNOW HOW I GOT THIS, DIDN'T YOU?
YEAH. COUPLE OF MONTHS AGO--JUST AFTER I'D MOVED THE SCHOOL OUT HERE FOR THE ROOM AND THE SECLUSION.
USED A NEUTOC CHARGER ON ME, THE LITTLE BASTARD.
BUT, ANGUS-- WHY?
REMEMBER WEAPONS CLASS, MERCY! NEUTOC CHARGERS ARE USED ONLY FOR RITUAL KILLS BY THE TROILIAN SECT OUT IN THE PHIBIAN COLONIES.
THE TROILIANS ARE A SMALL SECT. VERY BITTER, VERY INSULAR. AND VERY BIG ON VENDETTAS.
AND.. KARCH?

I MADE A DECISION BACK DURING THE MARTIAN CAMPAIGN OF '04. IT COST SOME OF OUR MEN THEIR LIVES. TROILIANS, IT SEEMS ONE OF 'EM WAS KARCH'S FATHER.

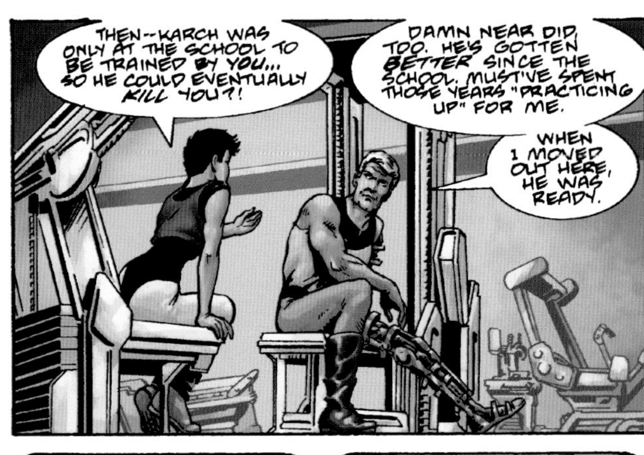
THEN--KARCH WAS ONLY AT THE SCHOOL TO BE TRAINED BY YOU... SO HE COULD EVENTUALLY KILL YOU?!
DAMN NEAR DID, TOO. HE'S GOTTEN BETTER SINCE THE SCHOOL. MUST'VE SPENT THOSE YEARS "PRACTICING UP" FOR ME.
WHEN I MOVED OUT HERE, HE WAS READY.

THEN HE JUST WAITED FOR ME TO GIVE HIM THE OPENING--JUST LIKE I TAUGHT HIM.

BUT-- I HAD ENOUGH LEFT TO PUT A HOLE OR TWO IN HIM, TOO. THINK THAT SURPRISED HIM. HE TOOK OFF, ANYWAY.
BY NOW, THOUGH, HE'S LICKED HIS WOUNDS. HE CAN BIDE HIS TIME.

BECAUSE MY WOUNDS...WELL, THE DOCS DON'T KNOW IF THE LIMBS'LL EVER REGENERATE.
SO HERE I SIT.

FIVE YEARS AGO, ANGUS WOULD'VE ALREADY TRACKED KARCH DOWN AND DRESSED OUT HIS CARCASS. BUT NOW...

ANGUS, I WOULDN'T WANT TO GET IN THE WAY, BUT DO YOU THINK I COULD TAG ALONG-- WHEN YOU'RE READY TO MOVE ON HIM, I MEAN?

I WAS THINKING OF STARTING TOMORROW, MERCY.

KARCH-- WE WERE SENT TO END THIS LONG DELAY. YOUR WOUNDS ARE HEALED--KILL THE OLD MAN AND HAVE DONE WITH IT.

"OLD MAN"? THIS IS ANGUS MCKEE! EVEN CRIPPLED, HE'S DEADLIER THAN THE THREE OF YOU PUT TOGETHER.

ONLY ANGUS COULD'VE GIVEN ME THESE WOUNDS.

MCKEE KILLED YOUR FATHER AND HIS MEN, KARCH. YOU'RE THE ONLY TROILIAN WHO CAN ANSWER FOR THAT! YOUR DUTY REQUIRES--

I KNOW DAMN WELL WHAT MY DUTY REQUIRES-- BETTER THAN YOU COULD EVER KNOW.
NOW SHUT UP AND LEAVE ME TO MY WORK.

I CLOSE MY MIND TO THEM AND BREATHE DEEP THE YUCCATA'S FUMES.
I CAST MY THOUGHTS OUT AGAIN... REACHING FOR ANGUS.

THERE HE IS. BUT SOME-THING IS WITH HIM-- SOMETHING POWERFUL. IT'S VAGUE, YET SOMEHOW FAMILIAR.
WITH ANGUS, I CAN TAKE NO CHANCES. SOON THIS IMAGE WILL CLEAR, THEN I'LL KNOW HOW TO MOVE.
PATIENCE, FATHER. IT'S ALMOST TIME.

NEXT MORNING, OUR HASTILY PREPARED SHIP IS ARCING TOWARDS *BEI*, THE SMALLEST OF VITRIUS'S MOONS.

ANGUS HAS LOOKED INTO TROILIAN LORE. HE SAYS THAT, ON BEI, KARCH WOULD BEST BE ABLE TO PERFORM SOME NECESSARY RITES FOR A TROILIAN *RITUAL KILL*.

I TRY TO PICTURE KARCH COOLLY PLANNING ANGUS'S DEATH. I STRUGGLE TO FIND A REASON FOR IT.

ANGUS.. HOW DID KARCH'S FATHER DIE?

I'VE BEEN WONDERING WHEN YOU'D ASK ABOUT THAT.

IT WAS ON *LISSI*.. THE REBEL ASSAULT ON OUR *SPACEPORT* THERE.

WE'D BEEN FIGHTING FOR DAYS. IT WAS A PIVOTAL SHOW, AND WE WERE *LOSING* IT.

"OUR SHIPS AND GROUND BATTERIES WERE NOTHING TO THEIR CRUISERS. MY OWN BATTERY WAS JUST THE *LAST* TO TAKE A DIRECT HIT.

"THROUGH THE SMOKE, I COULD SEE A CRUISER CLOSING ON THE PORT. BUT ONE OF OUR FIGHTERS FLOATED NEAR IT, HELPLESS AND DISABLED.

"THE FIGHTER HAD A CREW OF SEVEN. THERE WERE 1,375 PEOPLE IN THE PORT. I SAID A PRAYER AND PUNCHED THE *RAIDON* GUNS."

SOMEHOW, THEY FIRED. THE BLAST TOTALED THE CRUISER. IT ALSO ATOMIZED OUR FIGHTER.
THE CREW HAD BEEN *TROILIAN*. KARCH'S DAD WAS ITS CAPTAIN.

WE WON THE BATTLE. I EVEN GOT DECORATED FOR MY ACTIONS.
ANGUS-- YOU MADE THE RIGHT CHOICE.

HELL, MERCY. I KNOW THAT. DOESN'T CHANGE ANYTHING FOR THOSE MEN, DOES IT?

WE ARRIVE ON BEI AND MAKE STRAIGHT FOR THE TRICOST FORESTS. IT'S THERE THAT KARCH WOULD SEEK THE SECLUSION AND STRANGE FAUNA HE'D NEED FOR HIS RITUALS.

HE WON'T BE TOO FAR IN--AFTER ALL, HE'S NOT EXPECTING ANY COMPANY.

AND HE'D BE RIGHT ABOUT THAT, MERCY, IF NOT FOR YOU. I...

...I NEVER HAD MUCH OF A FAMILY, MERCY-- NOT TO SPEAK OF.
BUT... IF I WERE TO HAVE A DAUGHTE I'D...

HELL, LISTEN TO ME YAMMER. GETTING NERVOUS IN MY OLD AGE, I GUESS.
COME ON. LET'S END THIS THING.

OKAY-- YOU FLANK ME WIDE. I'LL SAIL STRAIGHT AHEAD. THAT'S SURE TO FLUSH HIM.
SINCE I'M COMING TO *HIM* THIS TIME, HE'LL HAVE TO MEET ME FACE TO FACE, SO WE CAN GET HIM ***CROSSED.***

I JUST HOPE HE'LL ***SEE*** THAT AND NOT PRESS A FIGHT.
DON'T COUNT ON IT, ANGUS. WHO KNOWS *WHAT* RULES HE'S PLAYING BY?

I MEAN, HE'S OUT TO KILL THE MAN WHO TRAINED HIM. HE HAS TO BE *CRAZY*! HE SHOULD BE... SHOULD BE...
YOU TRYING TO CONVINCE ME OR YOU, MERCY?
BUT KARCH *IS* PLAYING BY RULES-- *TROILIAN* RULES OF HONOR, OF PRIDE. WE'VE BOTH DRAWN ARMS FOR *LESS* OF A REASON: MONEY.

WHAT? THAT'S
DICULOUS,
GUS. WHAT
E DO IS
THIN THE
AW. WE'RE
NOT--
THE *LAW?* WHEN DID YOU GET *THIS* REVERENCE? I DIDN'T SEE IT SEVEN YEARS AGO.

AND SINCE THEN, I'LL BET YOU'VE *BROKEN* THE LAW GOING FOR *BOUNTIES* AS OFTEN AS I HAVE.
NO, MERCY. I THINK WE ONLY EVOKE "THE LAW" WHEN WE NEED TO JUSTIFY OUR *OWN* THIRST FOR VIOLENCE.

ANYWAY, THIS HAS NOTHING TO DO WITH THE LAW. NOT TO KARCH. AND NOT TO ME.
LET'S MOVE.

AS HE PUSHES INTO THE FOREST, ANGUS WOULD STILL LOOK TO ME LIKE THE *INDESTRUCTIBLE WARRIOR* HE'S ALWAYS BEEN--BUT FOR THE CRIPPLED *LEG* HE DRAGS BEHIND HIM.

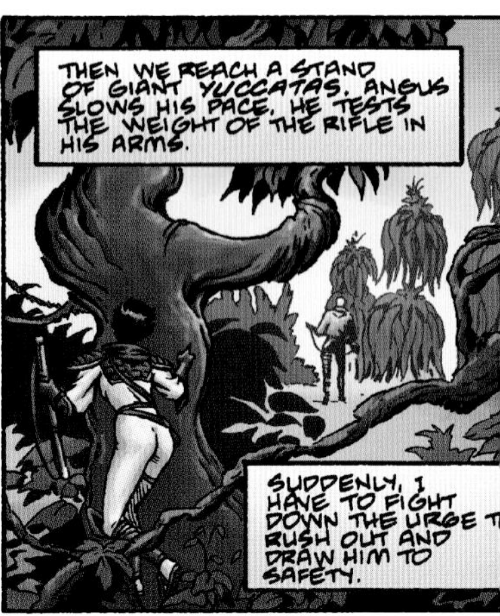
THEN WE REACH A STAND OF GIANT *YUCCATAS*. ANGUS SLOWS HIS PACE. HE TESTS THE WEIGHT OF THE RIFLE IN HIS ARMS.
SUDDENLY, I HAVE TO FIGHT DOWN THE URGE T
RUSH OUT AND DRAW HIM TO SAFETY.

THEN, IT'S TOO LATE FOR SAFETY.
THAT'S *FAR ENOUGH*, ANGUS. YOU SHOULD'VE STAYED HOME.

THERE, AT LEAST, YOU COULD HAVE BEEN BURIED BY FRIENDS.

IT TOOK *STONES* FOR YOU TO COME HERE, ANGUS. FOR WHAT IT'S WORTH, I'M SORRY THIS HAS TO BE.
THESE THREE WILL SERVE AS *WITNESSES* TO THIS PURGING KILL.
WHENEVER YOU'RE READY.

NO, KARCH!

YOU'RE NOT GOING TO DO THIS! I WON'T LET YOU KILL ANGUS.

OH, MY GOD.

MERCY.

SO THAT WAS MY VISION.
WHO'S THIS WOMAN, KARCH? WHY DO YOU--?
SHUT UP, DAINON!

MERCY, PLEASE LISTEN. I'VE SWORN AN OATH TO MY PEOPLE. FOR THEIR HONOR, AND IN THEIR NAME, ANGUS MUST DIE--BY MY HAND.
I CAN'T BREAK THIS PLEDGE--FOR ANYTHING...OR ANYONE.

BUT I BEG OF YOU--I PLEAD--FOR THE SAKE OF WHAT WE ONCE SHARED--WALK AWAY FROM THIS.

WHY DID I COME HERE? WAS IT REALLY TO HELP SAVE ANGUS...

...OR WAS IT JUST TO SEE THIS FIRE OF KARCH'S ONCE AGAIN? WHAT DID I HOPE TO FIND HERE?

HE HASN'T CHANGED--THE SAME PASSION--THE SAME PRIDE--STILL BURNS IN HIM. AS I KNEW IT WOULD.

I'M SORRY, KARCH. I... I CAN'T...

ENOUGH! THIS WOMAN IS NOTHING TO YOUR TASK, KARCH. I'LL--
DAINON NO--!

SPANG
BLAM

BRAKKA BRAK
NO, YOU FOOL RUN!

BOOM BOOM

ANGUS?
I'M FINE, MERCY. BUT KARCH--
VOOOOSH!

DAIVON AND THE OTHERS WERE FOOLS TRYING TO FIGHT WHEN CROSSED BY THE LIKES OF ANGUS AND--AND MERCY.
MERCY-- WHY ARE YOU HERE? HOW CAN YOU UNDERSTAND WHAT THIS IS ABOUT?

DO YOU KNOW HOW TROILIANS ARE TREATED BY THE STAR SYSTEM? HOW WE WERE SWEPT LIKE SO MUCH DIRT, INTO A GRIMY BACK CORNER OF THE GALAXY?
OR HOW OUR PEOPLE HAVE ALWAYS COUNTED AS NOTHING TO THEM...

...UNTIL THE WAR CAME AND THEY NEEDED US TO FIGHT FOR THEM? AND MY FATHER-- POOR, SIMPLE MAN. HOW EAGER HE WAS TO GO.
NO. NO TEARS, MARIA-- THE VALOR WE'LL SHOW IN BATTLE WILL WIN OUR PEOPLE RESPECT IN THE EYES OF THE ENTIRE SYSTEM.

AND YOU, KARCH-- CARE FOR YOUR MOTHER WHILE I'M GONE. YOU'LL BE THE SOLDIER HERE AT HOME, UNDERSTAND?
YES, POPPA.

THOSE WERE HIS LAST WORDS TO ME. I WATCHED HIM AND HIS DREAM SOAR INTO THE STARS, WHERE THEY WERE BOTH VAPORIZED IN THE NAME OF THE SYSTEM THEY SERVED.
NOT A TRACE WAS LEFT BEHIND OF THE MAN OR HIS VISION.

BUT WE WON'T VANISH SILENTLY, FATHER. I'LL CARVE YOUR MEMORIAL ON THE CORPSE OF THE "HERO" WHO KILLED YOU.

Chapter 4

HE'S GOT A FEW MINUTES ON US. HE'LL ALREADY BE IN THE TUBES SOMEWHERE.
HE PICKED A DAMN GOOD SPOT FOR THIS.

WE'LL HAVE TO SPLIT UP AGAIN AND HOPE TO FLUSH HIM OUT LIKE LAST TIME.
SPLIT UP? IN HERE? ANGUS, I CAN'T LET YOU--

USE YOUR HEAD, MERCY. WE MATCH TACTICS TO TERRAIN, REMEMBER?
NOW, I'LL TAKE THE TRANT LINES. YOU HIT THOSE TUBES.

MERCY KNOWS I'M RIGHT. SHE MOVES OFF. GOOD. SHE'LL BE SAFE. BECAUSE YOU'RE JUST AFTER ME, AREN'T YOU, KARCH?

YOU KNEW WE'D SPLIT UP, AND YOU'RE JUST WAITING FOR A CLEAR SHOT FROM UP IN THOSE PIPES, AREN'T YOU? THAT'S WHERE I'D BE.

SINCE WE ALREADY FACED OFF ON BEI, YOU'RE FREE TO TAKE ME ANY WAY YOU CAN. BUT WHEN I DON'T GIVE YOU AN OPEN SHOT FROM THE PIPES...

...YOU'LL MOVE TO THAT LIFT PLATFORM, WON'T YOU? IN FACT, YOU'LL BE MOVING RIGHT ABOUT... NOW.

WHICH MEANS I'D BETTER GET UP THERE FIRST.

DAMN THIS CRIPPLED SIDE OF MINE! ONE DAY IT'LL GET ME--

GOOD TRY, ANGUS..

--AT LEAST YOUR MIND WAS SHARP RIGHT TILL THE END

KRAKA
KRAK
KRAK

OH, MY GOD.

KARCH! NO!!

ANGUS? ARE YOU..?
I'M... UNH... BETTER THAN I SHOULD BE, MERCY.
DAMN. DIDN'T KNOW THIS OLD MAN COULD STILL DUCK THAT FAST!
YOUR SHOTS DROVE HIM BACK UP THE PIPES.

I'LL MANAGE HERE, YOU GET ON HIS BUTT-- DON'T LET HIM SET UP! PRESS! PRESS! GOT IT?
I'VE GOT IT, ANGUS.

NOW IT'S JUST THE TWO OF US. AND IF IT COMES TO KILLING, AM I READY TO--?

HUK

WHAM
WHUMP
WHUMP
IT LOOKS LIKE KARCH IS, ANYWAY.

SPLAK

NOT GOOD. THESE ARE THE BOWELS OF THE PLACE. SOME OF THE ENGINE WORKS STILL PUMP AND GRIND HERE, FILLING THE SPACE WITH NOISE, FUMES, AND HUGE, ROVING SHADOWS.
KARCH COULD BE ANYWHERE DOWN HERE.

KARCH-- LISTEN. I-I DON'T WANT THIS FIGHT. I DON'T THINK YOU DO, EITHER.
BUT IF YOU DON'T STOP THIS ONE OF US WILL DIE HERE.

LEAVE ANGUS ALONE! CAN'T YOU SEE THERE'S NO REASON FOR YOU TO--
THERE'S REASON ENOUGH TO THE TROILIANS MERCY.

DAMN. IN THIS RACKET, I CAN'T LOCATE HIS VOICE.
WHAT REASON? ALL YOU'LL GAIN IS MORE HATRED AND SCORN FROM THE WHOLE STAR SYSTEM!
MAYBE IF YOU'D KNOWN MY FATHER, MERCY, MAYBE THEN YOU'D UNDERSTAND.

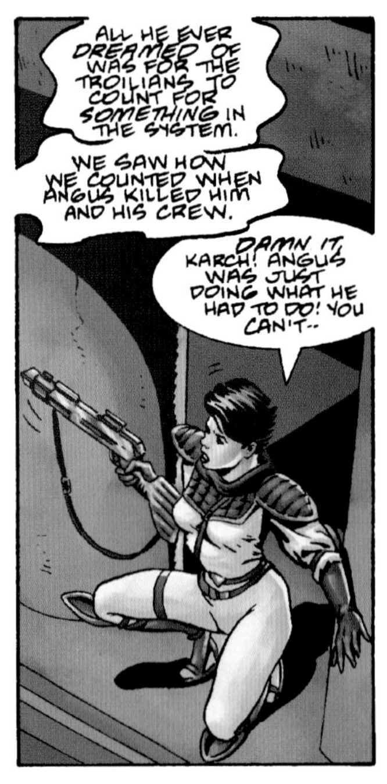
ALL HE EVER DREAMED OF WAS FOR THE TROILIANS TO COUNT FOR SOMETHING IN THE SYSTEM.
WE SAW HOW WE COUNTED WHEN ANGUS KILLED HIM AND HIS CREW.
DAMN IT, KARCH! ANGUS WAS JUST DOING WHAT HE HAD TO DO! YOU CAN'T--

THEY GAVE ANGUS A DAMN MEDAL, MERCY...

...THEY SANG HIM THEIR PRAISES,
AND WHY NOT...?

...AFTER ALL HE'D ONLY KILLED SOME LOUSY TROILIANS.
THAT'S WHAT WE MEANT TO YOUR SYSTEM, MERCY. THAT'S WHAT WE'VE ALWAYS MEANT.

THIS ISN'T AN ACT OF REVENGE, MERCY. IT'S A STATEMENT OF WORTH: THE TROILIANS WILL NOT BE THE TRASH OF THE SYSTEM ANYMORE.
I'M GOING BACK TO FINISH THIS NOW.

NO, KARCH. NO, YOU'RE NOT.

MURDER WON'T WIN THE TROILIANS ACCEPTANCE FROM THE SYSTEM, KARCH.
FOR THE LAST TIME, I'M TELLING YOU...I'M--I'M BEGGING YOU...
...STOP. STOP THIS NOW, OR I'LL--

YOU UNDERSTAND NOTHING, MERCY!
I'VE SWORN TO MY PEOPLE AN OATH BIGGER THAN MY LIFE--OR ANGUS'S...

...OR YOURS.
HIS SPEED IS IMPOSSIBLE-- OR DID I HESITATE IN FIRING?

GIVING YOU UP WAS THE HARDEST THING I'VE EVER DONE, MERCY.
BUT I DID IT, BECAUSE, AS A TROILIAN, I HAD TO--

--THE BLOOD OF MY FATHER DEMANDED IT!

HOW COULD YOU EVER UNDERSTAND SUCH A NEED?
DID YOUR FATHER DIE NEEDLESSLY.. FOOLISHLY--?
KRAK!

HAVE YOU SPENT YOUR WHOLE LIFE TRYING TO ATONE FOR HIS "SIN" OF BLINDLY TRUSTING THE SYSTEM?
KRAKA KRAKA KRAKA
KARCH WAS ALWAYS BIGGER, STRONGER.

NO, OF COURSE NOT. SO HOW COULD YOU LEARN TO SEE BEYOND YOUR OWN WANTS-- TO DENY YOUR OWN HEART?
BUT WITH HIS PASSIONS, HE MAY FORGET ONE OF ANGUS'S LESSONS AFTER ALL...

BUT--THAT'S WHAT I'VE HAD TO DO. THAT'S WHY I HAVE TO DO THIS.
...ONE OF THE FIRST ONES: KEEP YOUR HEAD IN A FIGHT, USE YOUR SURROUNDINGS...

GOODBYE, MERCY.
MAY GOD FORGIVE ME.
...AND TIMING...

...TIMING IS EVERYTHING.

WHOOSH!

KRUMPF

MAY GOD FORGIVE US *BOTH*, KARCH.

MERCY?

H--HERE, ANGUS.

WAIT THERE, KID...

LOOK AT US, MERCY-- LOOK AT THE RESULTS OF OUR LIFE'S WORK.
WE'RE VIOLENT PEOPLE. WE CONSUME EACH OTHER LIKE SHARKS AT FEEDING...
...AS IF WE KNOW NO OTHER WAY.

SOMETIMES I FEEL LIKE I'M MISSING SOMETHING INSIDE ME-- SOMETHING BURIED OR FORGOTTEN. YOU EVER FEEL THAT WAY, MERCY?

WELL, I HOPE YOU FIND THAT SOMETHING, MERCY, WHATEVER IT IS.
BECAUSE THIS...

...THIS ISN'T ENOUGH.

The End

THICKER THAN BLOOD
RANDALL '89

Story and art
RON RANDALL

Lettering
STEVE HAYNIE AND DAVID JACKSON

Chapter break art
RON RANDALL WITH CHRIS CHALENOR

WHEN PHOENIX **MELTED DOWN** IN '14, ALCON IMMEDIATELY SHUT DOWN ALL CONSTRUCTION ON NEW "PHASE 27" POWER PLANTS. IN **NEW GELAPH,** THAT MEANT THEY LEFT BEHIND A HALF-BUILT, TREACHEROUS RAT HOLE.

THE CITY POLICE POSTED A WARNING SIGN OR TWO AND FORGOT THE PLACE. THE CITY'S RIFFRAFF, HOWEVER, FOUND THE SIGHT IRRESISTIBLE.

WHICH MEANS THERE'S USUALLY A HEALTHY **BOUNTY** OR TWO SLINKING AROUND THERE.

THAT'S USEFUL INFORMATION WHEN YOU'RE A HUNGRY **TREKKER** LOOKING FOR HER NEXT MARK.

EVENING, **GLEARY.** ALWAYS A PLEASURE TO CATCH UP WITH YOU.

TREKKER

CREATED, WRITTEN, AND DRAWN BY
RON RANDALL

LETTERED BY
STEVE HAYNIE

1

WELL. MERCY ST. CLAIR, ISN'T IT? PRETTY SLICK--PRETTY FAST, AREN'T YOU?
DID I SAY YOU COULD GET UP?

CALM DOWN, SWEETHEART. I JUST WANT TO...

I'M JUST GONNA...

NO, DAMN IT! I SAID --!
WHAM

HEY, SISTER...YOU STILL WITH US?

YEAH. YOU'RE GOOD, ALL RIGHT. PRETTY QUICK...PRETTY TOUGH.
AND YOU HAD ME, TOO. HAD ME COLD.

YOU KNOW WHAT YOU'RE MISSING, THOUGH?
YOU'RE LOOKING RIGHT AT IT.
K-CHAK
KILLER INSTINCT.

I THOUGHT YOU WERE TOUGHER THAN THIS.

AAAGH!
BLAM
HUNNGH!
OKAY, GLEARY-- LET'S SEE THAT "KILLER INSTINCT."
3

YAAH!
WHUNK
KRANG
...I CAN'T BELIEVE THIS --BAGGED BY SUCH AN *AMATEUR!*
SHUT UP, GLEARY.
NO, I *MEAN* IT! YOU SHOULDA SEEN HER *FREEZE* ON THE TRIGGER.
IT WAS SLOPPY-- *UGLY.*
POLICE 23 PRECINCT
YOU BETTER TRIGGER FASTER THAN *THAT* NEXT TIME YOU'RE OUT THERE, SWEETASS-- UNLESS YOU'VE GOT SOME KIND OF DEATH WISH! YOU *HEAR* ME?
MERCY--COME IN HERE A MINUTE, WILL YOU?

HERE, MERCY. I HAD FRANK PUNCH UP YOUR CREDITS FOR GLEARY. IT'S NONE TOO BIG, THOUGH.
YOU, UH... NEED ANY CASH?
NO, UNCLE ALEX.
THANKS, BUT I'M FINE.

ARE YOU? THIS IS YOUR FIRST BOUNTY SINCE YOU GOT BACK TO THE CITY, MERCY. QUITE A LONG DRY SPELL, WASN'T IT?
I'VE JUST BEEN... GETTING REORIENTED, ALEX, THAT'S ALL.

MERCY--WHAT GLEARY SAID ABOUT YOU HESITATING OUT THERE. I NEED TO KNOW--IS IT TRUE?

I SEE.
WHAT IS IT, MERCY? WHAT'S WRONG?

LOOK--YOU KNOW I'M NOT CRAZY ABOUT YOU BEING A TREKKER. BUT AS LONG AS YOU ARE ONE, YOU CAN'T AFFORD TO LOSE THAT EDGE I USED TO SEE IN YOU.
YOU KNOW THAT TOO, MERCY...
...IT'S DANGEROUS ENOUGH OUT THERE WITHOUT--
ALEX--DON'T TALK TO ME LIKE I'M SOME ROOKIE IN YOUR COMMAND!
I KNOW WHAT I'M DOING.
I HOPE SO, MERCY. BECAUSE I'D RATHER HAVE A NIECE WHO'S A GOOD TREKKER...
...THAN A NIECE WHO'S A DEAD TREKKER.
5

THAT LITTLE TREKKER'S GONNA GET HERSELF KILLED. AND IT LOOKS LIKE SHE MAY TAKE ME WITH HER.
THESE HARD CASES HAVE BEEN ASKING ABOUT THE RICCOVICI BUST I HELPED HER ON. AND THEY'RE GETTING CLOSE.
BY NOW I'VE FIGURED THEY MUST BE GUNS FOR GATEFISH STRAUSS--PROBABLY THE SINGLE WORST KINGPIN YOU CAN CROSS IN THIS TOWN--
I'M TAKING CHANCES TO TAIL THEM LIKE THIS, SLICK AS THEY ARE. BUT IF I CAN'T FIND A WAY TO POP THEM SOON, I'LL BE PRIME GAME IN THIS TOWN--
--AND SO WILL MERCY ST. CLAIR.
THERE, MERCY. THAT FEEL ANY BETTER?
IT DOES, MOLLY. THANKS. FOR THAT AND THE DINNER, TOO.
I COULDN'T ADMIT IT TO ALEX, THE WAY HE'D WORRY, BUT I AM LOW ON FUNDS NOW.
AND HE WAS ALSO RIGHT ABOUT MY LACKING AN "EDGE."
SOMETHING'S NOT RIGHT, MOLLY. SOMETHING'S NOT WORKING ANYMORE.
I DON'T KNOW WHAT IT IS--AND I DON'T KNOW WHY IT IS. BUT IT'S GOT ME WONDERING...

WHY DO I DO THIS?
IS IT REALLY STILL FROM A BELIEF THAT YOU HAVE TO MEET STRENGTH WITH STRENGTH, GUN WITH GUN?
OR HAS THIS JUST BECOME SOME BLOODY HABIT I CAN'T BREAK FROM? OR EVEN WORSE...
IS IT SIMPLY THAT THIS IS ALL I KNOW HOW TO DO?
MERCY...
HELL-- PROBABLY ALL THREE, RIGHT?
WHATEVER IT IS, MERCY, YOU'LL TRACK IT DOWN. AFTER ALL, THAT'S SOMETHING YOU'RE VERY GOOD AT, ISN'T IT?
THANKS, MOLLY. LOOK--DON'T MIND ME. IT MUST JUST BE THIS HEAD WOUND.
I'D BETTER GET IT TO BED. THANKS AGAIN. MY PLACE NEXT TIME.
GOOD NIGHT, MERCY.
"YOU LOOKING FOR SOMETHING, PIGEON...?"
7

MAYBE IT'S US YOU'VE BEEN AFTER, HUH?
YEAH. MAYBE YOU'VE BEEN FOLLOWING US.
YOU NEED A PROGRESS REPORT, LAZMUSI, IS THAT IT?

OKAY. HERE'S THE HOT FLASHES FOR YOU. ONE: WE KNOW IT WAS YOU ON THE RICCOVICI BUST. YOU AND SOME TREKKER GIRL NAMED ST. CLAIR.
TWO: THAT'S ALL WE NEED TO KNOW.
THREE: WE DON'T LIKE BEING TAILED.
NO...

WHUUUGH!
I JUST BET YOU DON'T.
YOU SON OF A BITCH--!

KRAK

GREAT, HAWKINS. NOW WE'VE LOST HIM IN THAT SLIMING ROT. AND I WANTED TO--
FORGET THAT PIG...

...WE'LL JUST TAKE IT OUT ON HIS GIRLFRIEND.
YIKES! CONTINUED NEXT ISSUE!

IT'S BEEN OVER THREE MONTHS SINCE I'VE KILLED A MAN. OVER FIVE SINCE I'VE DONE SO FOR PAY.
TO A TREKKER, THOSE ARE WORRYING FACTS— FACTS THAT MAKE YOU ASK QUESTIONS. AND THAT'S DANGEROUS.
QUESTIONS MAKE YOUR MIND WANDER. AND FOR A BOUNTY HUNTER, THAT'S A LUXURY...
FWAP!
...THAT CAN BE FATAL.
EASY, LADY— WE JUST WANT A LITTLE—
YEAH—I CAN GUESS WHAT YOU WANT...
...BUT I'M GONNA GIVE YOU WHAT YOU NEED.
TREKKER
CREATED, WRITTEN, AND DRAWN BY RON RANDALL
LETTERED BY DAVID JACKSON

WHAM
OOOF
THE MOVE DOES MY HEAD WOUND NO GOOD, BUT THE FEEL OF HIS RIBS GIVING IS WORTH IT.
hnn...
I'M A TREKKER, YOU JERKS!
YEAH, HONEY—
CRACK
WE KNOW.
FWHIS
WHUMP
hung!

YAAAAH-!
UUUH
PAK PAK
SCREW THIS-!!

HANKS.
THINK.
THAT IS YOU UNDER THAT STINK, ISN'T IT, LAZMUS!?
DAMN
GHT IT'S ME.
D IT'S THANKS YOU I TOOK
IS SLUDGE BATH.
IT SAVED MY LIFE AFTER THOSE GOONS JUMPED ME IN THE SLOOSH LEVELS AN HOUR AGO.

THEY'RE AFTER US BOTH SINCE I HELPED YOU BUST RICCOVICI. HELL, I SHOULD HAVE KNOWN BETTER.
ANYWAY, WHEN I FINALLY PULLED MYSELF OUT OF THE SOUP I KNEW WHERE THEY'D BE HEADED.
LOOKS LIKE WE BEAT 'EM BACK. FOR NOW.

WHAT I DON'T GET IS WHY HAS THE GATEFISH SENT FOUR HOT GUNS ON US JUST FOR BUSTING ONE OF HIS TRIGGERS?
SEEMS HEAVY HANDED, EVEN FOR GATEFISH STRAUSS.
WELL, I'VE CROSSED HIM IN THE PAST, LAZMUS!. MAYBE I'VE JUST GOT HIM AGGRAVATED AT ME.
ANTARI AP
3

SORRY TO HAVE DRAGGED YOU INTO IT, TOO, THOUGH.
YEAH—LET'S MAKE HIM SORRIER.
GET SOME ORDNANCE ON YOU, ST. CLAIR. YOU CAN'T FACE STRAUSS WITH THAT LITTLE POPGUN.

I'M GONNA SCRAPE THIS MUD OFF AND TRY TO GET SOME MEN. SEE YOU IN THE MORNING.
WATCH YOURSELF. THIS IS A NASTY BUNCH.
"NASTY"? LOOK WHO'S TALKING! LAZMUSI HAS ENOUGH TOXIC SLUDGE ON HIM TO SKAG A GOR-HORSE, AND HE WEARS IT LIKE A LEISURE SUIT.
I'M BEGINNING TO SUSPECT, ONCE AGAIN, LAZMUSI'S FERVENT DENIALS OF ANY MUTANT ANCESTRY.
MY MIND IS WANDERING AGAIN.

BUT THEN THE TUBE DOORS OPEN ON MY FLOOR AND I'M BROUGHT BACK TO ATTENTION: SOMETHING'S WRONG.

BEFORE I'VE REACHED MY DOOR, I PICK UP THE SUBTLE TANG IN THE AIR: ACID IN MY DOOR'S LOCKS.

TYPICAL ENTRANCE STYLE FOR GATEFISH'S FINEST.

WHAM
YIP?
SCUF...?
WAY TO GO, FIDO. WHAT'D YOU DO, OFFER THEM DINNER?
THEY'D REALLY GIVEN THE PLACE THE ONCE-OVER BEFORE COMING AFTER ME. BUT WHY? WHAT ARE THEY AFTER?
AND HOW DOES IT TIE IN WITH RICCOVICI? NONE OF IT MAKES ANY SENSE...
...EXCEPT LAZMUSI'S ADVICE TO ARM UP.
IT'S AN HOUR TILL DAWN AND MY HEAD WOUND IS THROBBING. MAYBE THAT'S WHY I SIT DOWN TO WAIT.
IT FEELS GOOD TO SIT.
IT'S A MISTAKE.
YIP?
5

YOU NEED NEW LOCKS, ST. CLAIR.
STRAUSS!
EASY! DO OLD LAZMUSI A FAVOR AND HEAR HIM OUT.
LISTEN TO YOUR FRIEND, MISS ST. CLAIR. WE NEED TO TALK.
TAKE MR. LAZMUSI OUTSIDE, WILLIS. I HAVE A LITTLE STORY TO TELL MISS ST. CLAIR.

AS EVERYONE LEAVES, I WATCH STRAUSS'S HAND FIDGET WITH THE MEDICHAIR HE'S BROUGHT. I'D LIKE TO SEE WHAT MAKES THE GATEFISH NERVOUS. AND WITH HIS GUNS OUTSIDE MY DOOR, LOOKS LIKE I HAVE LITTLE CHOICE.
AH, GOOD. ALONE. YOU SEE, MISS ST. CLAIR, I DO ADMIRE YOUR CAUTION AND DISTRUST.
I QUITE AGREE, IN FACT. I TRUST NO ONE. NOT ANYMORE.

I TRUSTED A FELLOW ONCE. RICCOVICI.
AND IT'S BROUGHT ME MORE PAIN THAN I THOUGHT I COULD FEEL.

I'D MADE HIM THE HEAD OF MY INTERNAL SECURITY, YOU SEE. NEAR THE CORE OF ALL MY OPERATIONS — AND MY FAMILY.
TO HIM, IT MUST HAVE SEEMED THE IDEAL POSITION... FOR BETRAYAL.
BECAUSE HE WANTED MORE THAN I GAVE HIM. SUFFICE IT TO SAY, HE WANTED TOO MUCH.

I WAS PREPARING TO HAVE HIM REMOVED, BUT HE MUST HAVE GOTTEN WIND OF IT. HE DISAPPEARED.
YET, IF THAT HAD BEEN THE LAST I'D HEARD FROM HIM, I WOULD HAVE BEEN HAPPY. IT WASN'T.

YOU SEE, BEFORE HE LEFT, RICCOVICI BOUGHT HIMSELF A LITTLE NSURANCE LEVERAGE, THE MESSAGE SAID. "INSURANCE." THAT'S WHAT HE CALLED IT...

...WHEN THE SON OF A BITCH POISONED MY DAUGHTER.

THE SYMPTOMS MOUNTED, JUST AS HE'D CALLED THEM. RICCOVICI KNOWS HIS POISONS. AND, OF COURSE, HE HAD THE ONLY ANTIDOTE.

I COULD DO NOTHING. AND RICCOVICI KNEW IT. HE KNEW WHAT MY CHRISTINA MEANS TO ME. WE ARRANGED A MEETING.

I WAS PREPARED TO DO ANYTHING, TREKKER—TO MAKE ANY DEAL TO SAVE MY LITTLE GIRL.
A LOCATION WAS SET—TERMS FIXED... HE WOULD BRING THE ANTIDOTE...

...AND THAT'S WHEN YOU BUSTED HIM, ST. CLAIR.

I HAD MY MEN TRACK DOWN EVERYTHING HE'D HAD ON HIM WHEN ARRESTED—CLOTHES, HARDWARE... THE ANTIDOTE WAS NOWHERE.
CURIOUSLY, THOUGH, ONE WEAPON WAS ALSO MISSING. HIS DISTINCTIVE FRAK GUN. YOU REMEMBER THE PIECE?
7

YEAH. CUSTOMIZED JENKERS. VERY FLASHY. BUT I TURNED IT INTO IMPOUND WITH THE REST OF HIS STUFF. DIDN'T YOUR MEN—
OF COURSE THEY CHECKED. THERE'S NO RECORD OF IT, ST. CLAIR. NOT A TRACE.

SO YOU THOUGHT I MIGHT HAVE IT. WELL, NOW YOU KNOW I DON'T, RIGHT?
SO WHY-

THAT GUN MEANS MY DAUGHTER'S LIFE, TREKKER. AND YOU'RE GOING TO FIND IT FOR ME.
AM I? AND WHY, EXACTLY?
BECAUSE I HOLD YOU MAINLY TO BLAM FOR ITS LOSS

BECAUSE YOU HAVE BOTH THE GREAT TALENT AND CONNECTIONS TO DO SO. AN UNCLE ON THE FORCE, I BELIEVE.

BUT MOSTLY, YOU'LL DO IT FOR CHRISTINA.
LOOK AT HER ST. CLAIR. SHE THIRTEEN YEAR OLD... THE ONLY SWEET AND PURE THING I'VE GOT IN THIS WORLD...
...AND I'M LOSING HER FAS THESE DAMN TUB WON'T KEEP HE ALIVE MUCH LONGER.
YOU'LL DO IT FOR HER, MISS ST. CLA BECAUSE IT'S THE DECENT THING TO AND DESPITE YOURS

...THAT'S WHAT YOU ARE, AT CORE: DECENT.
CAREFUL, STRAUSS. I MAY DISAPPOINT YOU.

BAH! I KNOW YOU TOO WELL. I KNOW THAT HEART OF YOURS. IT'S YOUR GREAT WEAKNESS AS A TREKKER, YOU KNOW.
I'VE ALWAYS SUSPECTED THAT IT HAS SOMETHING TO DO WITH YOUR GIVEN NAME, MISS ST. CLAIR. WHAT DO YOU THINK...

...MERCY?
I'LL BE IN TOUCH.
CONCLUDED NEXT ISSUE.

HAVERSON, WE'RE GOING TO TALK.
WE ARE? ABOUT WHAT?
A GUN. ONE I'M SURE YOU'LL REMEMBER.
MALOY'S
BAR
IT WAS A CUSTOMIZED JENKERS. YOU WERE HANDLING IMPOUND WHEN I BROUGHT IT IN ON THE RICCOVICI BUST. REMEMBER?
I REMEMBER THE BUST. BUT NO, THERE WAS NO JENKERS.
NO RECORD, YOU MEAN. I SAW YOU TOOK CARE OF THAT. WHAT'D YOU DO WITH IT?
YOU BETTER SCAT, LITTLE TREKKER. YOUR KIND'S UNPOPULAR ENOUGH WITH COPS WITHOUT YOU CALLING US LIARS AND THIEVES.
I'M NOT LOOKING TO CAUSE YOU TROUBLE, HAVERSON, BUT I NEED THAT GUN.
FIRE OFF! WHAT KIND OF TROUBLE YOU THINK YOU CAN BE? WHO'S GONNA TAKE SOME TREKKER'S WORD OVER MINE?! I'VE GOT TEN YEARS ON THE FORCE AND—
I THINK YOUR SUPERIOR, LT. ST. CLAIR, MIGHT. YOU SEE, MY NAME'S ST. CLAIR, TOO...
TREKKER
...MERCY ST. CLAIR.
WE MAY BE A COP AND A TREKKER, BUT MY UNCLE AND I ARE STILL PRETTY CLOSE. FAMILY, YOU KNOW.
NOW. WHERE'S THE GUN? OR DO I HAVE TO GET UNPLEASANT ABOUT THIS?
CREATED, WRITTEN, AND DRAWN BY RON RANDALL
1

ALL RIGHT, ALL RIGHT. I SOLD IT TO A **COLLECTOR**. IT WAS THE ONLY TIME. I NEEDED THE MONEY. FOR--

I DON'T CARE ABOUT THAT. WHAT COLLECTOR?

A GUY NAMED **FRANKS**. LIVES IN THE COMPTON AREA. YOU KNOW...

"...VERY UPTOWN."

HAVERSON WAS RIGHT ABOUT THAT. GUESS THIS IS THE KIND OF NEIGHBORHOOD YOU WORK IN RUNNING ERRANDS FOR A MOB BOSS LIKE **GATEFISH STRAUSS**.

...OR RATHER, FOR HIS **DAUGHTER**. I KEEP REMINDING MYSELF I'M DOING THIS FOR HER... THAT IT'S NOT HER FAULT SHE WAS **POISONED** BY **RICCOVICI**...

...AND THAT SHE'LL DIE IF I DON'T RETRIEVE THE **ANTIDOTE** HIDDEN IN THAT FANCY GUN OF HIS.

THEN I WORK ON CONVINCING MYSELF THAT MY **CHARITY WORK** DOESN'T MEAN **STRAUSS** WAS RIGHT WHEN HE SAID IT SHOWS MY **WEAKNESS** AS A TREKKER.

I'M NOT DOING SO WELL ON THIS ONE WHEN.

BAM
THE BROKEN GUN RACK TELLS IT ALL. I'VE BEEN A FOOL. STRAUSS MUST'VE HAD ME FOLLOWED.

GUESS HE DIDN'T WANT
ME TO TOUCH THAT
ANTIDOTE, KNOWING THE
POWER IT'D HOLD
OVER HIM.

MAYBE STRAUSS
THOUGHT I'D JUST
LET IT GO AT THAT.
MAYBE HE WOULD'VE
BEEN RIGHT...

...EXCEPT THAT FRANKS
PUT TOO MUCH VALUE ON
THAT DAMN GUN.
PFFT

LL RIGHT—
HOLD IT,
YOU—

—RICCOVICI?!!
FRAKA FRAKA FRAKA FRAKA
3

BEOW
SPAK
SPAK
THE JENKERS GIVES HIM THE CLEAR UPPER HAND IN FIREPOWER.

IT'S LOOKING LIKE STRAUSS WAS RIGHT: I'M ABOUT TO PAY BIG TIME FOR THIS CHARITY WORK...
VIP
VIP
TZING
...UNLESS...
CLICK'A CLICK
...I CAN'T BELIEVE IT. HE'S EMPTY.
WELL, RICCOVICI. JUSTICE AFTER ALL, I GUESS. I'M GETTING TIRED OF BUSTING YOU.
TELL ME ABOUT IT, ST. CLAIR. I WAS AFRAID THIS THING WAS LOW...

...THAT'S WHY I ALSO BORROWED THIS!

BLAM

—HELL, ST. CLAIR. I
EARD YOU'D LOST
OUR **EDGE.** GUESS...
HAT'LL TEACH ME TO
STEN TO VICIOUS
GOSSIP.

HOW DID YOU GET **OUT,** RICCOVICI?

STRAUSS SPRANG ME, OF COURSE, TO HAVE ME KILLED. BUT... I'M SLIPPERY.

THEN I'VE JUST... LAIN LOW TILL I COULD GET A **LEAD** ON MY **GUN.**

WHEN I HEARD STRAUSS HAD TALKED TO YOU, I KNEW WHO TO FOLLOW.

I'M FLATTERED, RICCOVICI.

GOOD, I HOPE **STRAUSS** WILL BE, TOO. I... WANT TO BE THERE WHEN YOU GIVE HIM THE GUN. I NEED TO SEE HIM... FACE TO FACE.

SURE, RICCOVICI. YOU TWO DESERVE EACH OTHER. I'LL SEE WHAT I CAN ARRANGE.

ELL. ONLY SLIGHTLY
MAGED, I SEE.
YEAH. I KNOW WHAT A DISAPPOINTMENT THAT IS TO YOU, GATEFISH.
RELAX, RICCOVICI. AS I PROMISED MISS ST. CLAIR, SHE CAN HAVE YOU. MY ONLY INTEREST HERE IS IN SAVING MY DAUGHTER...

...AND AS YOU KNOW, I'M GOOD TO MY WORD.
GIVE WILLIS THE GUN, MISS ST. CLAIR. AND THE ANTIDOTE . . . ?
IT'S IN THE GRIP.

AH. OF COURSE. HOW—
HEY! IT'S EMPTY!!
OF COURSE IT'S EMPTY! I INJECTED MYSELF WITH IT AS SOON AS I GOT THE GUN.
IT'S ALL IN ME, NOW. AND I'M THE ONLY ONE WHO KNOWS THE PROCEDURE TO GET IT OUT AGAIN.
CUT ME LOOSE, ST. CLAIR.
YOU GET IT, STRAUSS? I'M THE ANTIDOTE.
KILL ME...

ALL RIGHT... I'LL... I'LL...
NUH--NO!!
AAARGH

?GNNH? YOU... NEED A LITTLE HELP BEING... NOBLE? OKAY... GLAD TO OBLIGE...
WILLIS! SHOOT HIM! SHOOT!
BUT, BOSS-YOUR KID-?
SHOOT, I SAID! SHOOT, DAMN YOU!
ALL OF YOU-SHOOOOT!
NO.

BRAKKA
BRAKKA
BLAM
BLAM
G-GRAB THE BELT, YOU LITTLE PRIV-
PFFT
BY THE TIME WE REELED BACK TO THE LEDGE, STRAUSS REALIZED WHAT HE HAD DONE. HE JUST STOOD THERE. IN FRONT OF US ALL, HE'D BETRAYED HIS LAST PRETENSE OF ANY PERSONAL CODE OF HONOR.
7

FOR A THUG LIKE **STRAUSS**, THAT WAS ALL HE HAD LEFT. WHEN HE AND HIS GUNS TOOK OFF, THEY WENT SILENTLY. AND HE LEFT **CHRISTINA** BEHIND.

ALL I COULD THINK WAS— "MY GOD. WHAT KIND OF **MONSTER** WILL HE BECOME NOW?"

I DON'T KNOW, MERCY. THAT MAY BE SO. BUT LOOK AT IT THIS WAY— YOU DID SAVE THE **DAUGHTER**, RIGHT?

YES... SHE'S GOING TO BE FINE. THERE IS THAT.

AND I BROUGHT IN RICCOVICI. I DIDN'T BUNGLE THAT TAG LIKE I DID WHEN I ALMOST LOST **GLEARY**.

AS LAZMUS I WOULD SAY, I GUESS I LEARNED A LESSON ON THAT ONE.

MAYBE, MERCY. OR MAYBE IT WAS JUST THAT YOU HAD A BETTER REASON TO **ACT** THIS TIME.

WHAT DO YOU MEAN, MOLLY? BOTH THOSE HOODS WERE SCUM. BOTH WANTED TO KILL ME.
YES, BUT YOU WERE AFTER GLEARY FOR THE BOUNTY, WEREN'T YOU? WHEREAS CATCHING RICCOVICI MEANT SAVING AN INNOCENT GIRL'S LIFE.

MAYBE THAT MADE A DIFFERENCE FOR YOU.
HMMM. WELL...

...THAT'S A PRETTY KIND INTERPRETATION. A "MOLLY" INTERPRETATION.
BUT IT DOESN'T SAY MUCH FOR ME AS A TREKKER, DOES IT?

MAYBE YOU SHOULD THINK INSTEAD, THEN...
ABOUT WHAT IT SAYS ABOUT YOU AS A PERSON.

THE END

INTERLUDE 2: MERCY KILLING

Story and art
RON RANDALL

Colors
CARY PORTER AND RON RANDALL

Lettering
STEVE DUTRO

IT ALWAYS GETS STARTED-- REALLY STARTED -- WHEN IT GETS GOOD AND DARK.
WH-WHAT ARE YOU DOING? WHAT --

SOME FOLKS JUST FLAT AREN'T COMFORTABLE IN THE DARK.

LISTEN TO THE TERROR IN THAT VOICE. IT WASN'T THERE BEFORE I KILLED THE LIGHTS.
WHAT DO YOU WANT? WHAT MORE DO YOU WANT?

OH, NO. AT FIRST THERE WAS HATRED IN THAT VOICE.

HATRED, THEN ANGER. BUT THAT'S ALL GONE NOW.
NOW IT'S JUST THE TERROR.

LIKE THAT'LL DO ME ANY GOOD.

I'M DOING HER A FAVOR AND SHE DON'T EVEN KNOW IT.
WHAT DO I WANT?

NOTHING.

NOTHING YOU CAN GIVE ME.

THE CALL FROM UNCLE ALEX COMES AT 3 A.M. I'M GREETED AT THE SCENE WITH THE DIZZYING, FAMILIAR STENCH OF CARNAGE. AND THE MADDENINGLY FAMILIAR SIGHT OF COP SEARCHLIGHTS ROVING BLOODIED WALLS AND CEILING.
AS IF FINDING ANSWERS TO SOMETHING LIKE THIS WAS AS EASY AS SHINING A LIGHT ON IT.
THE REAL ANSWERS ALMOST ALWAYS COME IN THE DARK. AND THEY'RE NOT PLEASANT. I'VE FOUND ENOUGH OF THEM TO KNOW. I'M A TREKKER. MY NAME'S MERCY ST. CLAIR.
BIGGER MESS THIS TIME, ISN'T THERE?
THINK HE'S AFRAID WE AREN'T PAYING ATTENTION, UNCLE ALEX?
FOURTH MULTIPLE THIS MONTH. NO PATTERN TO THE VICTIMS YET. I'VE GOT MY PEOPLE WORKING DOUBLE, TRIPLE SHIFTS.
HE'S GOT MY DAMNED ATTENTION, MERCY. HE'S AFTER SOMETHING ELSE. BUT WHAT? WHAT DOES THIS GUY WANT?
TREKKER™
MERCY KILLING
I SEE THE STRAIN ON MY UNCLE'S FACE. HE'S TAKING SERIOUS HEAT ON THESE KILLINGS, OTHERWISE HE'D NEVER CALL A TREKKER IN ON AN OFFICIAL OPERATION LIKE THIS.
I'M A BOUNTY HUNTER. THAT MAKES ME ALMOST AS HATED BY THE COPS AS BY THE CRIMINALS.
BUT THERE'S NEVER BEEN ENOUGH COPS IN NEW GELAPH, AND IT'S ONLY GETTING WORSE.
LAB'S READY TO CLOSE IT UP, LIEUTENANT.
FINE, HARPER. GIVE US A MINUTE.
I CHECK OUT THE WOUNDS CAREFULLY, NOTING EVERY DETAIL. MAYBE MY STREET CONTACTS WILL RECOGNIZE SOMEBODY'S "STYLE" IN THIS.
I PROMISE MYSELF I'LL END THIS SOON. AFTER ALL, ALEX IS...

...ALL THE FAMILY I'VE GOT, OLD SPORT.
AND SOMETIMES IT GETS PRETTY TEDIOUS, DOESN'T IT?
SURE COULD USE SOME COMPANY, COULDN'T WE?
WHAT IS IT, THEY STILL DON'T HAVE TIME FOR ME?
WELL, IT WOULDN'T BE THE FIRST TIME.
YER MORE TROUBLE THAN YER WORTH, YA SCRAWNY PRIV! IF I SEE YOUR FACE AGAIN...
FORGET IT, YOU SLIMY SHEEG RAT. I'D HAVE TO BATHE FOR A WEEK.
PACKING Co.
BEAT IT, YA SICKO! I'VE HAD ENOUGH OF YOU HACKIN' UP GOOD MEAT. KNIFER AS GOOD AS YOU ONLY MAKES A MESS LIKE THAT 'CAUSE HE ENJOYS IT.
NOW EVEN THE COPS IGNORE ME. WHA THE HELL ARE THEY DOIN'? LIK THEY GOT LIVE TO LIVE OR SOMETHING.

WELL, YOU HAVE TO LIVE OUR LIFE, ON'T YOU?
YES, MOLLY, BUT EVERY MINUTE COUNTS ON THIS ONE. IF YOU'D SEEN UNCLE ALEX'S FACE LAST NIGHT...
LOOK, YOU'VE STILL GOT TEN MINUTES BEFORE YOU MEET THAT CONTACT, RIGHT? TIME ENOUGH FOR A BAVARIAN ROLL. EAT.
I ONLY HOPE THIS GUY CAN MAKE SOMETHING FROM THESE WOUNDS. THEY WERE SO DISTINCTIVE. DEEPER, CLEANER THAN ANY STREET KNIFER COULD DO.
PRECISE, LIKE HE KNEW JUST HOW MUCH PAIN EACH CUT WOULD...
OOPS. SORRY. I DIDN'T MEAN TO...
FORGET IT. IT MUST BE HARD TO JUST TURN IT OFF. I KNOW.
SO HOW ARE THINGS WITH YOU AND DETECTIVE DESMOND?
THEY AREN'T, MOLLY. WE'RE JUST TOO DIFFERENT, I GUESS. HE NEEDS... TOO MUCH LIGHT.
EXCUSE ME?
WELL, THAT'S WHAT PAUL SAYS. THAT I'M TOO "DARK" FOR HIM, TOO HARD. LIKE I CAN JUST TURN OFF THE STREET WHEN WE GET TOGETHER JUST SO HE CAN BE COMFORTABLE.
I CAN'T. I WON'T. IF THAT MAKES ME DARK, THEN FINE. I'LL BE DARK.
NO, YOU WON'T, MERCY. WHAT YOU DO -- YOUR WORK -- IS HARD, AND HARSH. BUT YOU, "DARK"? I KNOW BETTER.
BUT YOU ARE A NGEROUS CENTRIC, MOLLY NDOWNER.
ANYWAY, ME FOR MY LE "BUSINESS ETING." THANKS R THE BREAK-FAST.
AS ALWAYS, MERCY HASN'T THE TIME FOR SENTIMENT. THAT WOULD RUN THE RISK OF SOMEONE SAYING TO HER...
...YOU'RE WEAK.

...A COWARD AND A WEAKLING. SOMEBODY SHOULD PUT YOU OUT OF YOUR MISERY.
BETTER IDEA: LET'S PUT YOU OUT OF YOUR MISERY.
THAT WON'T PROVE ANYTHING. YOU'RE STILL A COWARD, YOU BASTARD.
DAMN HIM! WHERE'S THE FEAR? HIS EYES HAVE NO... WAIT.
YES. OF COURSE.
WELL, HERO, HOW DOES THIS GRAB YOU?
...ELLIE...
DADDY...
YES. THAT'S IT. PERFECT.
KRISH
THANK GOD MY GUY WAS RIGHT. HE KNEW THOSE WOUNDS CAME FROM A BENTON CLEAVER AND THEN REMEMBERED HEAR-ING ABOUT THIS PSYCHO MEAT MAN SKULKING THE STREETS.
ONCE I HAD A DESCRIPTION AND AN AREA TO WORK WITH, THE SPOTTING WAS A MATTER OF TIME.

END OF THE LINE, EDDIE.
HOLD IT, TREKKER. DROP THE GUNS OR I'LL--

I'M NOT HERE TO TALK WITH YOU, EDDIE.
ARGH!

UUHH
WHUMP

BLAM
BLAM

DID YOU...
ONLY ONE WAY TO FIND OUT. STAY HERE.

BE CAREFUL. HE SAID HE HAD OTHER GUNS ON HIM.
HE'LL NEED THEM.

FINALLY.
ABOUT TIME.

DAMN. SHE SHOT ME UP GOOD. HURTS LIKE... HELL, TOO...

MAYBE... MAYBE *NOW* I CAN...

NO... NOT EVEN NOW. *STILL*... JUST A... LOSER.
GOD. IF... I COULD PRAY...

...I'D PRAY FOR ...AN *ANGEL*...

...A *DARK ANGEL*...

...OF MERCY.

END

TREKKER™
TRIAL BY FIRE
KESEL

Story and art
RON RANDALL

Colors
MOOSE BAUMANN AND RON RANDALL

Lettering
RON RANDALL

Chapter break art
RON RANDALL WITH KARL KESEL AND MOOSE BAUMANN

NEW GELAPH.
2226.
THE MOVES ARE FAMILIAR, ALL WELL PRACTICED.
ANTARI APTS

BUT THAT DOESN'T ERASE THE DANGER.

WHENEVER TWO POWERFUL FORCES MEET...

...THE RESULTS CAN BE UNPREDICTABLE...

...VOLATILE...

...EXPLOSIVE.

THAT'S PART OF THE FASCINATION, OF COURSE.

HOW CLOSE TO THE FLAMES CAN YOU GET...

...BEFORE YOU GET BURNED?

TREKKER
IN THE END, THE FLAMES ALWAYS DIE AWAY. AND WHEN THAT HEAT IS GONE, YOU'RE LEFT FACING THE SAME QUESTION AS ALWAYS...
...IS THERE ANYTHING LEFT IN ITS PLACE...
...ANYTHING BESIDES THE COLD AND THE DARK?

Trial by Fire
by RON RANDALL
EEPT
--TECTIVES RESPOND, OVER. REPEAT: ALL DETECTIVES RESPOND.
CLEMONS. WHAT'S UP?
ANOTHER FIREBALL. DEEGAN DISTRICT. REPORT IMMEDIATELY TO--
PAUL IS UP AND DRESSING BEFORE THE ADDRESS HAS COME OVER THE BOX.
THE FORCE IS SO SHORT ON MANPOWER, VIRTUALLY EVERYONE'S ALWAYS ON CALL.

AND THEY'RE STILL DROWNING IN THE SCUM OUT THERE.
HEY, MERCY...
THAT'S WHERE TREKKERS COME IN.
...THAT SOUNDED LIKE YOUR UNCLE.
I KNOW. I'LL SEE YOU THERE.

PAUL AND I TAKE DIFFERENT ROUTES TO THE SCENE.
LICENSED BOUNTY HUNTERS ARE NOT WELCOMED BY THE POLICE.
UNLESS OF COURSE, ONE'S YOUR UNCLE. AND THE LIEUTENANT.
UNCLE ALEX!
MERCY?! HOW DID YOU GET WIND OF THIS SO FAST?
THE STENCH OF DEATH IS THICK. THERE'S TIGHTNESS IN MY UNCLE'S VOICE AND EYES.
POLICE
DO NOT CROSS · POLICE
ME?...I WAS JUST...PASSING BY...
UH-HUH. IF YOU SAY SO, MERCY.
ALEX, HOW--HOW MANY...?
153 DEAD. OVER 300 INJURED. ADD THIS TO THE TWO BLASTS LAST WEEK AND THE DEATH COUNT'S OVER 270.
AND MY PEOPLE ARE GETTING NOWHERE.

SO THIS TIME I WELCOME YOUR HELP, MERCY.
BUT UNDERSTAND--THIS ISN'T A TWO-BIT STREET PRIV YOU'RE AFTER. THIS ANIMAL'S A MASS MURDERER.
ONE WITH WEAPONS AND RESOURCES WE CAN'T SEEM TO TOUCH.
I CAN TAKE CARE OF MYSELF, ALEX. DON'T WORRY.
I AM WORRIED. THAT'S WHY I WANT YOU TO MEET--
--AIV BOOTH. ANOTHER TREKKER WITH A KNACK FOR TIMELY ARRIVALS, IT SEEMS.
I'D LIKE YOU TO WORK TOGETHER. MAYBE YOU'LL GET SOME RESULTS ON THIS THING.
SOUNDS REASONABLE TO ME, LIEUTENANT. WHAT DO YOU SAY, MS. ST. CLAIR, PARTNERS?
NO.
THANKS.
LOOK--IF IT'S THE MONEY, I'M WILLIN TO LIVE WITH 40%.
I KNOW THIS IS YOUR TURF HERE, MERCY. I'M NOT TRYING TO STEP ON ANY TOES.

I'LL BE IN TOUCH, ALEX.
MERCY--I WAS REALLY HOPING YOU'D WORK WITH ME HERE. I NEED THIS CREEP CAUGHT FAST.
PFFT
I'LL CATCH HIM, ALEX.
I DON'T NEED A DAMN CHAPERONE.
WOW.
SETTLE DOWN, BOOTH. THAT'S MY NIECE, REMEMBER?
SORRY, LIEUTENANT. NO OFFENSE MEANT.
MIND IF WE JUST WIPE THE SLATE CLEAN?

I HIT ALL MY CONTACTS, PRESSING THEM HARDER THAN EVER BEFORE.
I TELL MYSELF IT'S BECAUSE OF THE SCALE OF THE CASE. BUT IT'S MORE THAN THAT.
I PICTURE UNCLE ALEX TRYING TO FOIST THAT JOKER BOOTH OFF ON ME. I'M TRYING TO PROVE SOMETHING TO THEM, AND TO MYSELF.
MY RESULTS DON'T DO MUCH FOR MY CAUSE.
EVEN LAZMUSI HAS LITTLE TO OFFER.
SORRY, ST. CLAIR. TALK IS THERE'S SOME OFF-WORLD ANGLE TO THESE FIREWORKS, BUT I CAN'T MAKE THE CONNECTIONS.
MY GUYS ARE KEEPING THEIR EYES OPEN, THOUGH.
SPACE SMUGGLERS?
HARD TO SEE IT. THE BOMB SITES' GOT NO LINES TO ANY OUTFITS I EVER HEARD OF. IT DON'T ADD UP, ST. CLAIR.
IT WILL WHEN I'M DONE.
WHO YOU SELLING THAT TO, ME OR YOU?

IT'S A GOOD QUESTION. THE ANSWER HAUNTS ME ALL THE WAY BACK HOME.
TS
ANTAR
REMEMBER THE 270 DEAD. I REMEMBER THE *TIGHTNESS* IN NCLE ALEX'S VOICE.
BUT THAT MAKES ME REMEMBER *BOOTH*.
AND THAT MAKES ME *ANGRY*.
ND THAT MAKES E *CARELESS*.

GOOD EVENING, MS. ST. CLAIR. WE DO HOPE YOU'LL FORGIVE US BARGING IN LIKE THIS.
WE HEAR YOU'VE BEEN ASKING QUESTIONS. DANGEROUS QUESTIONS.
THAT DISTURBS US. WE'D LIKE YOU TO STOP.
YOU'VE HEARD OF THE JORDIAN CLUB, I ASSUME? NO?
WELL, JUST THINK OF IT AS OUR WAY OF SAYING "PLEASE."
AFTER ALL, WE'VE HEARD HOW STUBBORN YOU CAN BE. AND WE REALLY MUST MAKE A LASTING IMPRESSION ON THIS POINT.
AAAGH--!!
SKZZKT
GET HE DOWN! HER DO
OOOF!
DAMN-- SHE'S A TOUGH LITTLE KITTEN!
ALL RIGHT, BOYS, NOW I'M SURE MS. ST. CLAIR HAS--
WHO THE HELL ARE YOU?
OH, DEAR MORE DANGER QUESTIONS. PERHAPS WE H FINISHED YE

DON'T YOU SEE, MY DEAR? THERE ARE LARGE FORCES AT WORK HERE. AND WE SIMPLY WILL NOT TOLERATE--
MERCY?! MERCY! ARE YOU ALL RIGHT? I HEARD--
HANG ON! I'M--
BAM BAM
WHAT THE HELL--?
OW!
SON OF A--
OH, LORDY...
AND YOU WOULD BE...?
I--I'M THOMPSON RICHARDS. N-NEIGHBOR FROM UPSTAIRS. I'M A--A HISTORY PROFESSOR. I DEMAND--
A HISTORY PROFESSOR?
HAW! GUESS HE'S BEEN READIN' TOO MUCH ABOUT KNIGHTS IN SHINING DAMN ARMOR!
HEY! WATCH OUT--SHE'S--
PFFT
CRACK
GAAAAGH--!!

NORMALLY I'M NOT TOLERANT OF NOSY NEIGHBORS. PRIVACY'S HARD ENOUGH TO COME BY IN A FLIMSY DUMP LIKE THIS. BUT TONIGHT I'M IN A FORGIVING MOOD.
HUUGH--!
GAGH--!!
BLAMBLAM
THAT CHARITY, HOWEVER, DOESN'T EXTEND TO THE SKITE WHO JUST SCRAMBLED MY NERVOUS SYSTEM.
NO. WE NEED TO TALK.
THANKS, THOMPSON. BUT I DON'T REALLY THINK THIS IS YOUR LINE OF WORK, IS IT?
HEY, =OUCH= IT WORKED, DIDN'T IT?
BESIDES, WHAT'S A FEW BRUISES COMPARED WITH THE CHANCE TO PLAY GALAHAD TO MERCY ST. CLAIR?
THE HITTERS LEFT THEIR AIR CYCLES HOVERING. THEY WERE SURE I'D BE AN EASY MARK.
THEY WERE DAMN CLOSE TO BEING RIGHT.

I CRANK THE THROTTLE AND THE CYCLE SCREAMS INTO THE GRITTY NEW GELAPH SKY.
MY EYES NEVER LEAVE THE SKITE RIDING THE OTHER BIKE. SOMETHING'S WRONG ABOUT THE WAY THIS LITTLE SCENE HAS PLAYED OUT.
I DON'T PLAN ON LETTING THE ANSWERS GET AWAY FROM ME.

THE SKITE KNOWS THESE BIKES BETTER THAN I DO. BUT I KNOW THE CITY. I CUT ANGLES. USE THE HEAT UPDRAFTS. CLOSE THE DISTANCE.
SHE KNOWS IT, TOO.
SHE'S GOT A .387 FLAM. ENOUGH FIREPOWER TO TURN MY RIDE INTO METAL SHAVINGS IF I GIVE HER TIME.
SO I DON'T.

ALL RIGHT, QUEENIE-- STRAIGHT-TALK TIME. YOU PLAY AROUND WITH THAT PARTY WAND--THEN ONLY TAKE SHOTS AT MY AIR BIKE--
YOU WANT ME ALIVE. WHY?
DAMN IT, TWITCH, HOLD STILL! YOU WANT ME TO DROP YOU?
SORRY, ST. CLAIR...
AAAGH!
...BUT I'M LEAVING.
YOU CRAZY--
YOU DON'T KNOW THE STAKES HERE, TREKKER.
BELIEVE ME, YOU'RE WAY OUT OF YOUR--
--DEEEEPTH!

NO ANSWERS, AFTER ALL, JUST MORE QUESTIONS.
THE POLICE COME, GO THROUGH THEIR MOTIONS. THEN LEAVE WITH THE BODIES. AND THE SAME QUESTIONS.
YOU GOING TO BE ALL RIGHT, MERCY?
ONCE I GET THIS MESS FIGURED OUT I WILL.
THOSE PRIVS WERE ACTING THE PART OF STREET-GANG HITTERS. BUT NO REASON FOR A STREET GANG TO TOY AROUND WITH ONE TREKKER.
OR TO PLAY WITH MASSIVE FIREBOMBS.
THIS WAS ALL A SMOKE SCREEN. THERE'S MORE GOING ON HERE THAN I'M SUPPOSED TO KNOW.
YOU GOT THAT RIGHT, FIRECRACKER.
BOLT!
HELLO, MERCY. DELIGHTED TO SEE YOU, AS ALWAYS.
I SEE YOU'RE IN THE THICK OF THINGS AS USUAL. MAYBE I CAN HELP.
BOLT!--THE LAST THING I NEED RIGHT NOW IS TO HEAR YOUR SPACE-GAS THEORIES. WHY DON'T YOU JUST--
UH, MERCY-- WHO'S--
THIS SPACE CASE IS JASON BOLT. GO HOME, T.R. THE DAY I CAN'T HANDLE A NUT LIKE HIM IS THE DAY I HANG UP MY HOLSTER.

OKAY, BOLT. MAKE IT QUICK.
FAIR ENOUGH.
YOU KNOW WE AT **RIGEL** HAVE BEEN KEEPING AN EYE ON THE **GALACTIC COUNCIL** AND ALL THEIR SLEAZY DOINGS.
WE BELIEVE MANKIND NEEDS **BETTER** LEADERSHIP THAN **THAT** AS WE SPREAD INTO THE STARS.
CUT THE **SPEECH**, BOLT. I GET IT. YOU RIGEL JOKERS HAVE ABOUT AS MUCH USE FOR THE COUNCIL AS I DO FOR YOU.
WHAT'S THIS GOT TO DO WITH THESE **BOMBINGS**?

LOOK, FIRECRACKER. I KNOW HOW YOU REGARD RIGEL. ND **ME**, WHEN IT COMES TO THAT. BUT WE'RE ON YOUR SIDE. AND WE'RE SERIOUS ABOUT THIS. THE **COUNCIL'S** LINKED TO THE **BOMBINGS**.
WHAT?! YOU **ARE** CRAZY. WHY WOULD THEY--
YOU'VE HEARD OF THE **SH'ARN**, **MERCY?** THOSE SHADY ALIENS CONTROLLING THE URUS SECTOR?
WELL, THE **PUBLIC** MAY NOT LIKE THEM, BUT THE COUNCIL'S HAVING QUITE SENSITIVE NEGOTIATIONS WITH THEM. IT INVOLVES SOME LUCRATIVE **SPACE ROUTES** OUT THERE.
ANYWAY, RIGEL'S INTERCEPTED **CODED COMMS** BETWEEN THEM. AND THEY'RE TALKING ABOUT THE **NEW GELAPH BOMBINGS.**
WHY? WHAT CAN THEY POSSIBLY HAVE TO DO WITH **URIAN SPACE ROUTES?**

WE DON'T KNOW, YET. BUT WE HAVE FAITH IN YOURINCREDIBLE ABILITIES.
IF YOU WANT A **HAND**, I'D BE GLAD TO--
WHAT? YOU, TOO?!
"I COULDN'T **BELIEVE** IT..."

...I MEAN, FIRST IT'S UNCLE ALEX WITH THAT SLEAZY TREKKER BOOTH, AND NOW THAT CLOWN BOLT! TELL ME, MOLLY, DOES EVERYBODY THINK I'M HELPLESS?
BELIEVE ME, MERCY ST. CLAIR, "HELPLESS" IS ABOUT THE LAST WORD PEOPLE WOULD TAG YOU WITH!
BUT THAT'S NOT THE SAME AS ACCEPTING A FRIENDLY HAND ONCE IN A WHILE, IS IT?
MAYBE NOT. BUT THAT REQUIRES TRUST. AND TRUST DOESN'T COME EASY IN MY LINE OF WORK.
I SUPPOSE NOT. LOOK, MERCY, I KNOW HOW IMPORTANT THIS CASE IS TO YOU. AND THAT YOU WANT TO CLOSE IT ON YOUR OWN.
I ALSO KNOW YOU'LL MAKE THE RIGHT CHOICES FOR YOU, WHATEVER HAPPENS.
CAREFUL, MOLLY. THAT ALMOST SOUNDS LIKE WHAT BOLT SAID TO ME WHEN I BLEW HIM OFF.
OOPS, SORRY! ANYWAY, I'D BETTER GET BACK TO THE SHOP. THOSE FLUTES AND HORNS DON'T SELL THEMSELVES.
ARE YOU SEEING THE DASHING DETECTIVE CLEMONS TONIGHT?
YES--UNLESS A MIRACLE HAPPENS AND I CATCH A LEAD THIS AFTERNOON. WISH ME HAPPY HUNTING.
I WISH YOU A GOOD DINNER.

NEITHER OF US GETS HER WISH. EVERY CONTACT I FOLLOW COMES UP EMPTY.
EVERY TRACK LEADS TO A DEAD END.
I EXHAUST EVERY HOPE I HAVE AND AM LEFT WITH NOTHING TO SHOW FOR IT.
NOTHING BUT A KNOT OF FRUSTRATION IN THE PIT OF MY STOMACH.
I'M IN A LOUSY MOOD AT DINNER, EVEN BEFORE PAUL STARTS PRESSING AGAIN...
SO, HOW ABOUT IT, MERCY? ONE MONTH GETHER. YOU CAN SAY IT'S ON A "TRIAL BASIS" IF YOU LIKE. WHAT CAN IT HURT?
PAUL, YOU'RE NOT ON TRIAL. IT'S JUST THAT RIGHT NOW I'M NOT READY FOR...
THEN, SUDDENLY, THE WISHES KICK IN...
EXCUSE ME, MISS. GENTLEMAN SAID IT WAS URGENT.
Cafferty Towers— Tonight. L.
... AND DINNER IS EXCELLENT.
L. LAZMUSI.

PAUL INSISTS ON DRIVING. I AGREE BECAUSE IT SAVES TIME. WE PICK UP MY GEAR AND I CHANGE ON THE WAY TO THE TOWERS...
OKAY, PAUL, NOW YOU CAN CALL IT IN AND EVACUATE THE TOWERS.
BUT LEAVE THE ARSONIST TO ME, GOT IT?
I DON'T WAIT TO HEAR HIM ANSWER. THERE ARE 1,400 PEOPLE IN GAFFERTY TOWERS.
NOT REPORTING THE TIP UNTIL NOW PUTS ME IN THE SLING FOR ALL OF THEM IF I DON'T FIND...
CLINK
THERE.
PAUL--?
YOU GO RIGHT.
PAUL-- WHAT ARE YOU DOING HERE?!
YOU THINK I'D REPORT THIS NOW, JUST TO COVER MY OWN ASS?
LET'S MOVE. I'LL CALL HIM OUT.

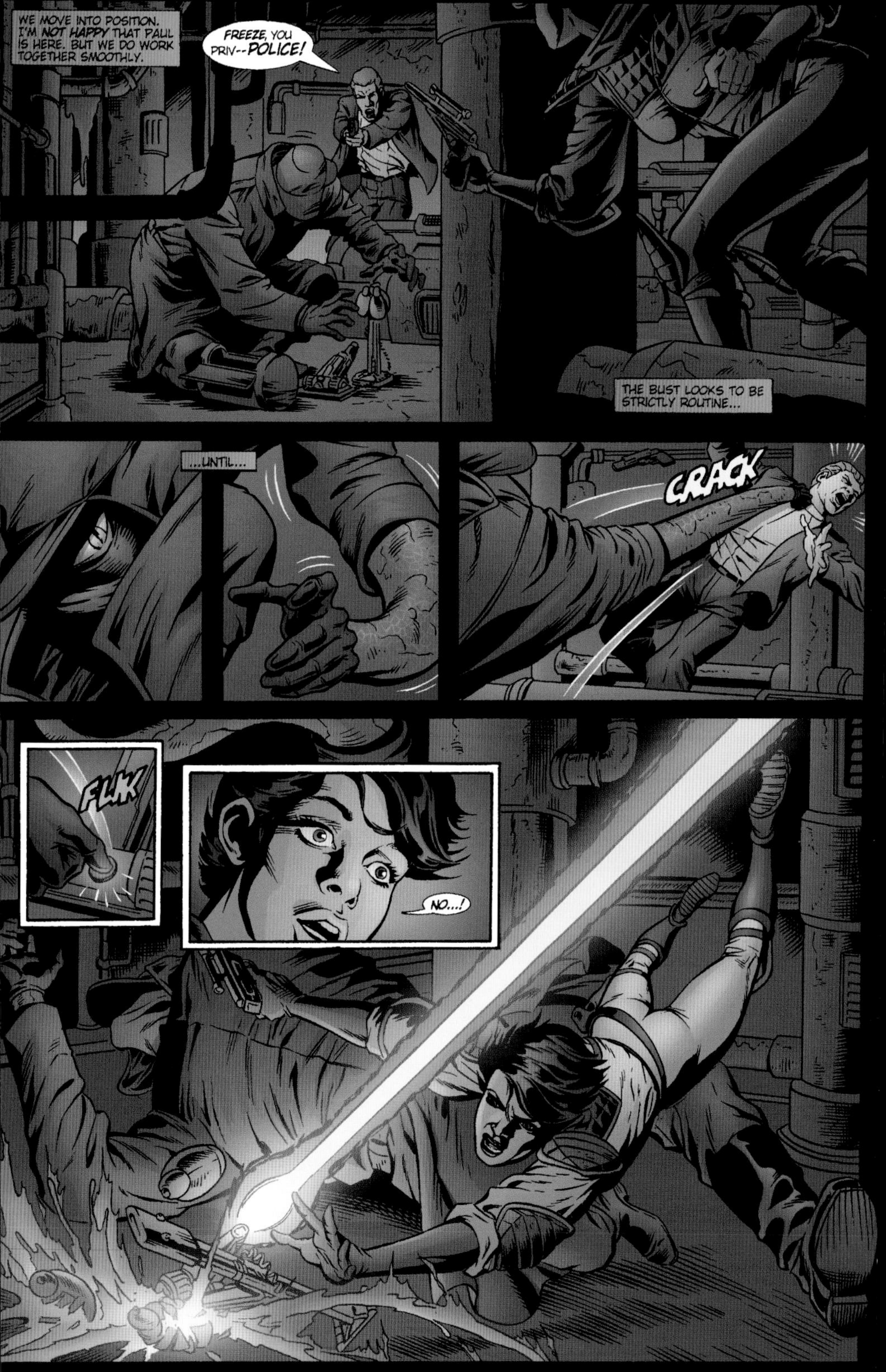
WE MOVE INTO POSITION. I'M NOT HAPPY THAT PAUL IS HERE. BUT WE DO WORK TOGETHER SMOOTHLY.
FREEZE, YOU PRIV--POLICE!
THE BUST LOOKS TO BE STRICTLY ROUTINE...
...UNTIL...
CRACK
FLIK
NO...!

SPILLING THE THERMALITE BEFORE THE MAGNA TORCH CAN FIRE IT SAVES THE BUILDING FROM BLOWING--
--NOW ITS FLAMING SPRAY JUST THREATENS TO BURN US UP.
AND THAT ISN'T THE WORST OF MY TROUBLES.
HE'S A DAMN SH'ARN--! THAT FOOL BOLT WAS RIGHT.
AND THAT HURTS EVEN WORSE THAN THE SH'ARN'S PUNCHES.
ALL RIGHT, UGLY-- I WANT SOME ANSWERS!
I THINK I CAN HELP YOU THERE, ST. CLAIR.

BOOTH--! HOW DID YOU GET HERE?!
EASILY ENOUGH, ST. CLAIR. I FOLLOWED YOU.
ODY WAS ING ME!
OF COURSE NOT. YOU'RE FAR TOO GOOD TO BE TAILED. SO, WHEN YOU REFUSED MY OFFER TO WORK TOGETHER, I HAD YOU ELECTRONICALLY TAGGED. MAKES TRACKING MUCH SIMPLER.
THE SKITE WITH THE JORDIAN WAND. SHE WAS MARKING ME FOR YOU.
YES. A SUCCESSFUL COLLABORATION BETWEEN OUR TWO GOVERNMENTS. AND YOU'VE BEEN QUITE AN EFFECTIVE PAWN AS WELL, ST. CLAIR.
NOW THE NEED FOR PRETENSE IS AT AN END.
A CHAMELEON BELT--!
OUR GOVERNMENTS ARE ENGAGED IN POTENTIALLY LUCRATIVE BUT CONTROVERSIAL NEGOTIATIONS OVER CERTAIN SPACE ROUTES.
KNOWLEDGE THAT A SH'ARN IS BEHIND THE DEATHS OF SO MANY HUMANS WOULD DESTROY THESE ARRANGEMENTS.
TO AVOID SUCH... EMBARRASSMENT, ALL TRACES OF THIS EPISODE MUST BE ERASED.

AND THE MOST DANGEROUS ELEMENT GOES FIRST, ST. CLAIR.

MERCY-- NO!

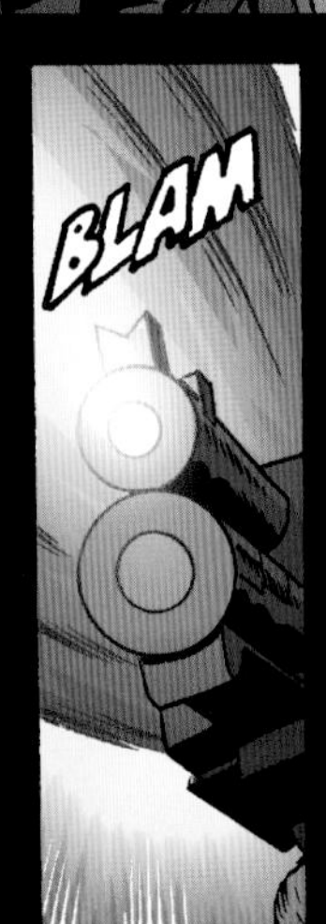

GRAAAGH!

SO--MY PEOPLE WANT ME DEAD NOW, DO THEY? FOOL.
THEY SENT ME.
PAUL...
I WAS ASSIGNED TO ELIMINATE SOME LEADING RESISTERS TO OUR PACT WITH THESE HUMANS. MY FIRST BOMB DID THAT. THE OTHERS WERE MERELY TO DISGUISE THAT PURPOSE.
AND NOW THAT MY USEFULNESS HAS ENDED, I'M TO BE CAST ASIDE? VERY WELL...
BUT IF I'M TO HAVE NO HERO'S HOMECOMING...
...THEN NEITHER SHALL YOU!!
AAAAGH!
ALL THAT HEAT... ALL THOSE FLAMES. AND ALL I FELT WAS COLD--

--COLD AND EMPTY.
HELL, I DON'T KNOW WHY I'M TALKING LIKE THIS. I'VE SEEN DEATH BEFORE.
THIS IS DIFFERENT, MERCY. PAUL LOVED YOU.
YES...HE DID. AND TO A DEPTH I NEVER REALLY KNEW--
--BECAUSE I DIDN'T FEEL THE SAME FOR HIM.
I DOUBT I'M EVEN CAPABLE OF IT.
OF COURSE YOU ARE, MERCY. DO YOU THINK PAUL WOULD HAVE LOVED YOU LIKE THAT IF YOU WEREN'T?
I DON'T KNOW, MOLLY. I WISH I COULD BE THAT SURE.
I ONCE TOLD PAUL HE WASN'T ON TRIAL WITH ME. NOW I WONDER IF THAT WAS A LIE.
IF IT WAS, THE ONE THING THAT'S CLEAR TO ME IS THAT HE PASSED HIS TRIAL BY FIRE.
AND FOR ME TO DESERVE THAT, I'LL HAVE TO PASS MY OWN TRIAL, ONE WAY OR ANOTHER, EVERY DAY.
THE END

SKETCHBOOK

SKETCHES, ART, AND COMMENTARY BY RON RANDALL

The first piece of "finished" *Trekker* art: This was the "pitch art" I presented to Mike Richardson and Randy Stradley when I originally proposed the series. They invited me to fashion the series just as I would most want to do it and, bless them, they went for it.

©'86 RON RANDALL
TREKKER for the cover of DHP#41.

Below are three spot illos for a *DHP* cover bullet, a Dark Horse trading card image, and another image from the "Scarmen's Burn" back cover. I, for one, find Mercy's face and features endlessly fascinating to draw from just about any angle or mood.

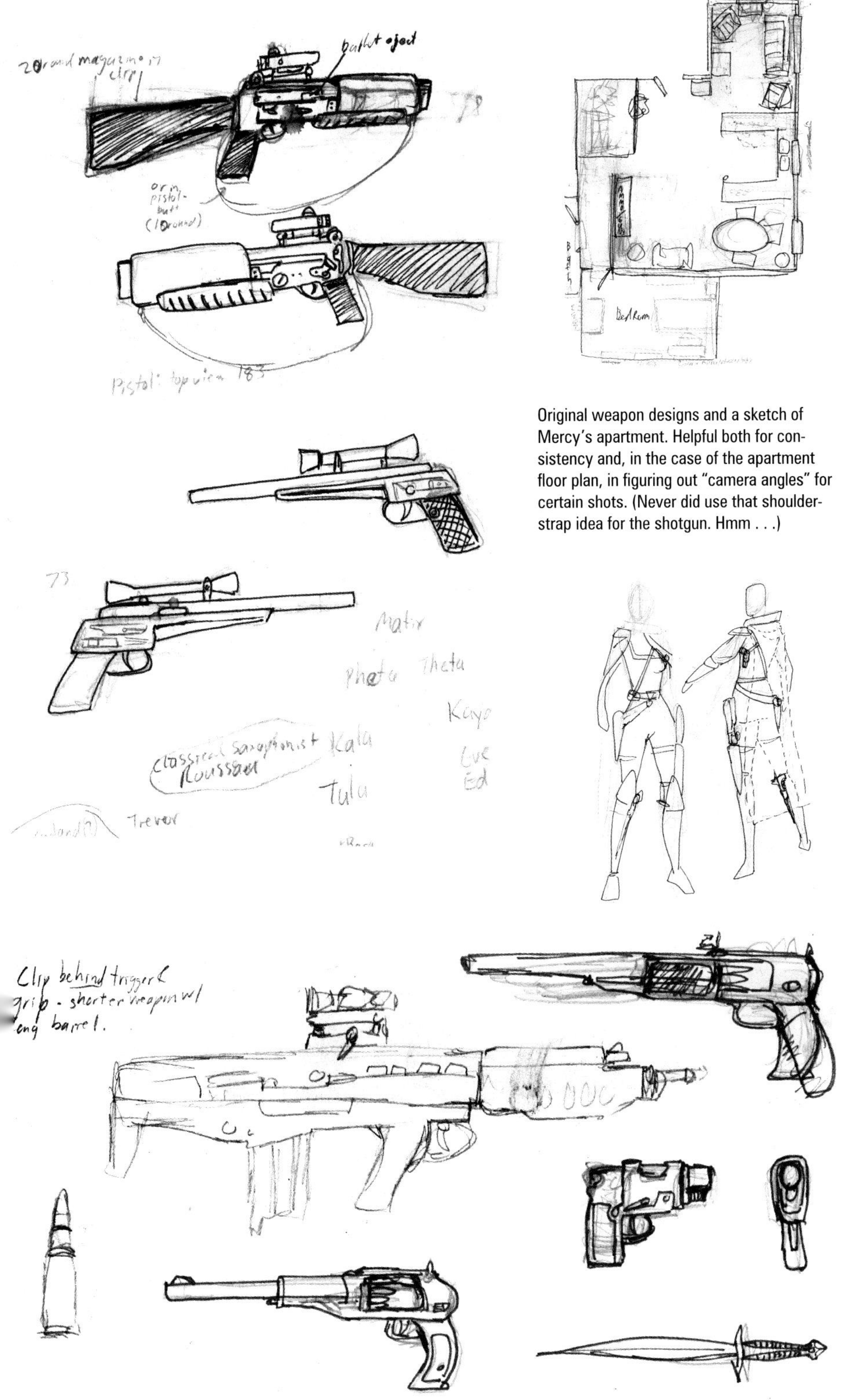

Original weapon designs and a sketch of Mercy's apartment. Helpful both for consistency and, in the case of the apartment floor plan, in figuring out "camera angles" for certain shots. (Never did use that shoulder-strap idea for the shotgun. Hmm . . .)

Some promotion pieces. Left column: A full-page house ad from the early Dark Horse days, a design for a comic shop–centric ad, and the back cover from the "Trail to Scarmen's Burn" story. The figure on the right was originally planned as a central image for a cover, but was ultimately used as part of an in-house Dark Horse lineup and later on the inside cover for the "Sins of the Fathers" story.

Some real, honest-to-goodness *sketches*. Top left: my very first, spontaneous sketch of Mercy, our Trekker. This is where I just let the pencil (and later the marker) flow across the page and saw what came out as I thought about a sci-fi action heroine. In this case, what came out was pretty close to a final design. That doesn't often happen. The rest of these are various outfit designs that you'll be able to spot in the preceding stories.

The fancy stuff: Top is the original wraparound cove for the "Sins of the Fathers" story. Editor Diana Schutz wisely suggested a simpler, bolder cover. Next is a drawing for an *Amazing Heroes* magazine swimsuit issue: Mercy and Molly on alien shores. And last, an unused cover for a potential "Thieves i the Temple" style story.

"THE TREKKER WITH GIRLS"

Before-and-after of a rare *Trekker* collaboration pinup. Mercy meets up with the Malibu Comics character Lester Girls from the *Trouble with Girls* series. And I was able to have my good friend and peerless comics creator Karl Kesel ink my pencils on the piece. If you want to have your art look really great, it's pretty simple: get Karl to ink it. (Karl also inked the cover from the "Trial by Fire" story in this collection.)

"THE TREKKER WITH GIRLS"

LESTER! I COULD USE A LITTLE HELP HERE!

WHAT–? OH.

GEE... AND THIS BOOK WAS JUST GETTING EXCITING...

RANDALL KESEL 10·31·91

LESTER™© JACOBS'N'JONES TREKKER™©RON RANDALL EVERY SINGLE LINE OF INK © KARL KESEL

Above: Two early versions of pages from "Trial by Fire." Sometimes you get a better idea for blocking out the action a bit late in the game. And you end up with some "almost pages."

Below: Two pencil pages from an unfinished short story. Abandoned stories are both sad and frustrating. And *that* is why I am now back to continue telling *Trekker*'s tale from the point where it leaves off in this collection. There's so much more to tell about Mercy St. Clair's journey, and it's time to be up to that task.

One of two bookend pages that ran in *DHP* #40.

RANDALL
Colwell

ABOUT THE AUTHOR

Ron Randall has worked for every major comics publisher in the United States, including Marvel, DC Comics, Image, and Dark Horse Comics, on properties as varied as *Spider-Man*, *Supergirl*, *Predator*, and *Star Wars*. *Trekker* is his own creation and his signature project. Returning to Dark Horse to continue telling Mercy St. Clair's ongoing tales is a highlight of his career. Ron is a founding member of Portland, Oregon's Periscope Studio, the largest collective of professional cartoonists in the country.

ACKNOWLEDGMENTS

Trekker would never have existed without a leap of faith and support from Mike Richardson and Randy Stradley at Dark Horse. My gratitude to them both always.

To the extent that *Trekker* is a series of any substance and value, I am everlastingly indebted to several generous companions along the way. Chief among them: David Clemenson and Curt Thayer for helping light the spark, Linda Nichenko for support above and beyond, Elisabeth Hummel for vision, Joe Kubert for setting the bar and showing how to leap it, Diana Schutz for her insights, and, inescapably, Duane and Peggy.

Standing atop the list of my collaborators are longtime lettering master Ken Bruzenak, who has been along from almost the first page and is still gracing *Trekker* with his unique touch, and Jeremy Colwell, whose formidable gifts as a colorist and patience as a collaborator are helping me to realize *Trekker*'s world more fully than I could have ever dreamed of. John Workman designed a *Trekker* logo that remains timeless, classic, and an absolutely perfect fit for Mercy's world of action and adventure. Lucy Bellwood contributed wonderful cover design ideas, and editor Jim Gibbons has lent enthusiasm and energy that have allowed this collection to sparkle.

Lyn, *Trekker* would not be back on the stands today without your infinite faith, patience, and support.

Thanks to the longtime loyal fans who've continued to keep the faith, and to all the readers along the way who have tried something new and found a connection in these pages. You guys are what gives it all meaning.

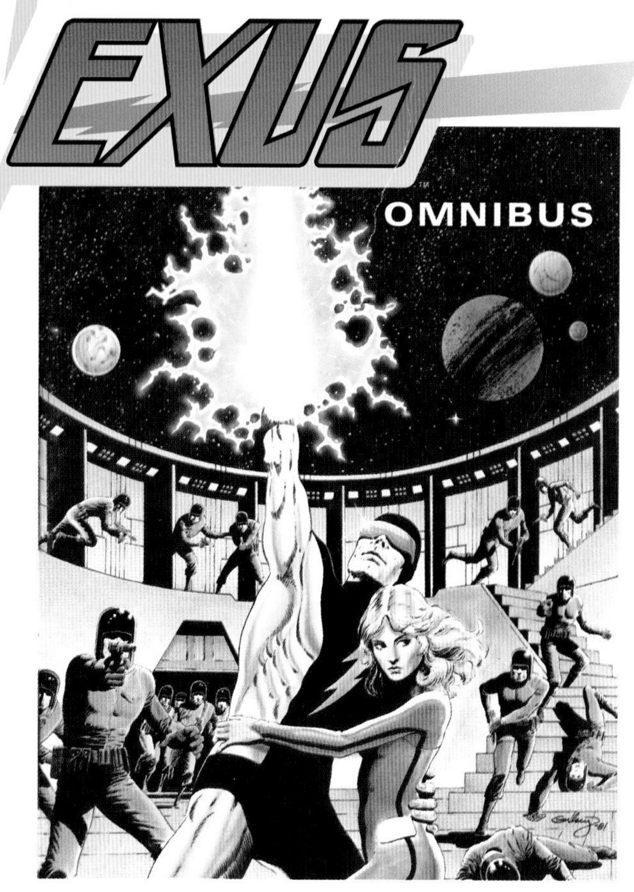

On the distant moon of Ylum, an enigmatic man is plagued by nightmares of the past. He dreams of real-life butchers and tyrants, and what they have done.

And then he finds them, and kills them.

The year is 2841, and this man is Nexus, a godlike figure who acts as judge, jury, and executioner for the vile criminals who appear in his dreams. He claims to kill in self defense, but why? Where do the visions come from, and where did he get his powers? Though a hero to many, does he have any real moral code? These are but some of the questions that reporter Sundra Peale hopes to have answered.

A multiple Eisner Award–winning series that defined the careers of acclaimed creators Steve Rude and Mike Baron, *Nexus* is a modern classic, now available in omnibus editions.

VOLUME 1	**VOLUME 2**	**VOLUME 3**	**VOLUME 4**
ISBN 978-1-61655-034-9	**ISBN 978-1-61655-035-6**	**ISBN 978-1-61655-036-3**	**ISBN 978-1-61655-037-0**

$24.99

AVAILABLE AT YOUR LOCAL COMICS SHOP OR BOOKSTORE!

To find a comics shop in your area, call 1-888-266-4226. For more information or to order direct:

On the web: DarkHorse.com • E-mail: mailorder@darkhorse.com • Phone: 1-800-862-0052 Mon.–Fri. 9 AM to 5 PM Pacific Time